P9-CDZ-061

WITHDRAW

Race Relations

OPPOSING VIEWPOINTS®

Race Relations

OPPOSING VIEWPOINTS®

Other Books of Related Interest

Race Relations

O P P O S I N G   V I E W P O I N T S®

Mary E. Williams, *Book Editor*

David L. Bender, *Publisher*
Bruno Leone, *Executive Editor*
Bonnie Szumski, *Editorial Director*
Stuart B. Miller, *Managing Editor*

OPPOSING
VIEWPOINTS®
SERIES

Greenhaven Press, Inc., San Diego, California

Cover photo: John Foxx Images; EyeWire Studios

Library of Congress Cataloging-in-Publication Data

Race relations : opposing viewpoints / Mary E. Williams, book
   editor.
      p.   cm. — (Opposing viewpoints series)
   Includes bibliographical references and index.
   ISBN 0-7377-0519-1 (pbk. : alk. paper) —
   ISBN 0-7377-0520-5 (lib. bdg. : alk. paper)
      1. United States—Race relations. 2. United States—Race
   relations—Government Policy. I. Williams, Mary E., 1960–
   II. Series: Opposing viewpoints series (Unnumbered).

E184.A1 R316   2001
305.8'00973—dc21   00-037561
                                                        CIP

Copyright ©2001 by Greenhaven Press, Inc.
Printed in the U.S.A.

No part of this book may be reproduced or used in any
form or by any means, electrical, mechanical, or otherwise,
including, but not limited to, photocopy, recording, or
any information storage and retrieval system, without
prior written permission from the publisher.

Every effort has been made to trace the owners of copyrighted material.

Greenhaven Press, Inc., P.O. Box 289009
San Diego, CA 92198-9009

E
184
.A1
R316
2001

"Congress shall make no law... abridging the freedom of speech, or of the press."

First Amendment to the U.S. Constitution

The basic foundation of our democracy is the First Amendment guarantee of freedom of expression. The Opposing Viewpoints Series is dedicated to the concept of this basic freedom and the idea that it is more important to practice it than to enshrine it.

KELLY LIBRARY
EMORY & HENRY COLLEGE
EMORY, VA 24327

Contents

Why Consider Opposing Viewpoints?

"The only way in which a human being can make some approach to knowing the whole of a subject is by hearing what can be said about it by persons of every variety of opinion and studying all modes in which it can be looked at by every character of mind. No wise man ever acquired his wisdom in any mode but this."

John Stuart Mill

In our media-intensive culture it is not difficult to find differing opinions. Thousands of newspapers and magazines and dozens of radio and television talk shows resound with differing points of view. The difficulty lies in deciding which opinion to agree with and which "experts" seem the most credible. The more inundated we become with differing opinions and claims, the more essential it is to hone critical reading and thinking skills to evaluate these ideas. Opposing Viewpoints books address this problem directly by presenting stimulating debates that can be used to enhance and teach these skills. The varied opinions contained in each book examine many different aspects of a single issue. While examining these conveniently edited opposing views, readers can develop critical thinking skills such as the ability to compare and contrast authors' credibility, facts, argumentation styles, use of persuasive techniques, and other stylistic tools. In short, the Opposing Viewpoints Series is an ideal way to attain the higher-level thinking and reading skills so essential in a culture of diverse and contradictory opinions.

In addition to providing a tool for critical thinking, Opposing Viewpoints books challenge readers to question their own strongly held opinions and assumptions. Most people form their opinions on the basis of upbringing, peer pressure, and personal, cultural, or professional bias. By reading carefully balanced opposing views, readers must directly confront new ideas as well as the opinions of those with whom they disagree. This is not to simplistically argue that everyone who reads opposing views will—or should—change his or her opinion. Instead, the series enhances readers' understanding of their own views by encouraging confrontation with opposing ideas. Careful examination of others' views can lead to the readers' understanding of the logical inconsistencies in their own opinions, perspective on why they hold an opinion, and the consideration of the possibility that their opinion requires further evaluation.

Evaluating Other Opinions

To ensure that this type of examination occurs, Opposing Viewpoints books present all types of opinions. Prominent spokespeople on different sides of each issue as well as well-known professionals from many disciplines challenge the reader. An additional goal of the series is to provide a forum for other, less known, or even unpopular viewpoints. The opinion of an ordinary person who has had to make the decision to cut off life support from a terminally ill relative, for example, may be just as valuable and provide just as much insight as a medical ethicist's professional opinion. The editors have two additional purposes in including these less known views. One, the editors encourage readers to respect others' opinions—even when not enhanced by professional credibility. It is only by reading or listening to and objectively evaluating others' ideas that one can determine whether they are worthy of consideration. Two, the inclusion of such viewpoints encourages the important critical thinking skill of objectively evaluating an author's credentials and bias. This evaluation will illuminate an author's reasons for taking a particular stance on an issue and will aid in readers' evaluation of the author's ideas.

As series editors of the Opposing Viewpoints Series, it is our hope that these books will give readers a deeper understanding of the issues debated and an appreciation of the complexity of even seemingly simple issues when good and honest people disagree. This awareness is particularly important in a democratic society such as ours in which people enter into public debate to determine the common good.

Those with whom one disagrees should not be regarded as enemies but rather as people whose views deserve careful examination and may shed light on one's own. Thomas Jefferson once said that "difference of opinion leads to inquiry, and inquiry to truth." Jefferson, a broadly educated man, argued that "if a nation expects to be ignorant and free . . . it expects what never was and never will be." As individuals and as a nation, it is imperative that we consider the opinions of others and examine them with skill and discernment. The Opposing Viewpoints Series is intended to help readers achieve this goal.

David L. Bender & Bruno Leone,
Series Editors

Greenhaven Press anthologies primarily consist of previously published material taken from a variety of sources, including periodicals, books, scholarly journals, newspapers, government documents, and position papers from private and public organizations. These original sources are often edited for length and to ensure their accessibility for a young adult audience. The anthology editors also change the original titles of these works in order to clearly present the main thesis of each viewpoint and to explicitly indicate the opinion presented in the viewpoint. These alterations are made in consideration of both the reading and comprehension levels of a young adult audience. Every effort is made to ensure that Greenhaven Press accurately reflects the original intent of the authors included in this anthology.

Introduction

*"The story of race at the end of the 20th century and into
the 21st century is a story of conflicting viewpoints."*
—Advisory Board to the President's Initiative on Race

In a 1995 *Washington Post* opinion poll, participants were
asked, "How big a problem is racism in our society today?"
Sixty-seven percent of surveyed blacks stated that racism was
a big problem, while only 38 percent of whites agreed. In
another 1995 *Washington Post* survey, 36 percent of whites
felt that "past and present discrimination is a major reason
for the economic and social problems" facing blacks, but
more than half of the African American respondents agreed
that discrimination remained a significant barrier to blacks'
success.

Numerous polls and surveys taken throughout the 1990s
reveal that whites and minorities often hold sharply contrasting opinions about racial discrimination and race relations.
According to President Bill Clinton's Advisory Board on
Race, whites and people of color see "racial progress so dif-
ferently that an outsider could easily believe that whites and
most minorities . . . see the world through different lenses."
Often referred to as the racial "perception gap," this difference of opinion between whites and nonwhites is especially
noticeable when examining public opinion on governmental
attempts to redress racism and discrimination. For example,
recent surveys indicate that between 60 and 75 percent of
whites oppose affirmative action policies—measures that increase minority representation in the workplace by including
race as a factor in hiring decisions—while 65 to 70 percent of
minorities support them. In addition, a Gallup poll reveals
that 65 percent of blacks supported a 1997 proposal for Congress to apologize for slavery, while 67 percent of whites opposed such an apology.

What accounts for such differences of opinion between
whites and minorities? Certainly, most Americans today
seem to detest bigotry and claim to support the ideal of
racial equality. Yet, for some reason, most people of color

see racial discrimination as an ongoing impediment, while a majority of whites believe that much of the problem of racial intolerance in the United States has been solved. Many analysts maintain that this racial perception gap is a result of the different life experiences that whites and minorities have. As legal analyst Richard Delgado states, "White people rarely see acts of blatant or subtle racism, while minority people experience them all the time." Psychologist John Dovidio agrees: "We [whites] tend to see racism as not a problem and particularly not a problem for us. [However], people of color experience . . . subtle biases on a daily basis. They see a discrepancy between what we say overtly, which is about fairness, justice, and equality, and the subtle biases that pervade our society."

These biases, many point out, are evident in white people's reactions to people of color. Minorities report that whites are often anxious in their presence: Salesclerks follow them around in stores, worried that they might shoplift something; taxi drivers refuse to give them rides; police pull them over to check their cars for weapons or drugs; whites seem fearful when they have to stand near black or Latino men in elevators. Such occurrences, experts maintain, are often the result of negative racial stereotypes that have permeated American society for generations. These stereotypes include the beliefs that racial minorities are less intelligent and more prone to criminal behavior than whites are. People are exposed to such stereotypes early in life, and they can become part of a person's worldview even though he or she may genuinely believe that prejudice is wrong. "In America," writes author David Shipler, "a child has only to breathe and listen and watch to accumulate the prejudices that govern ordinary thought. Even without willful intention, with no active effort, a youngster absorbs the images and caricatures surrounding race. Nobody growing up in America can escape the assumptions . . . that attach themselves to one group or another."

Intensifying the lingering problem of stereotypes, many commentators contend, is the fact that many American communities remain segregated. As a result, numerous people go through life with no significant or long-term contact with those of other races, and they are not afforded the perspective that could be gained from cross-racial interaction. Whites, for example, do not usually experience much prejudice in their own lives or know many people who have experienced racial discrimination, so they may conclude that racism is not much of a problem today. On the other hand, minorities' encounters with racial discrimination make it more difficult for them to believe that whites could support the goal of racial equality. Moreover, repeated experiences with racism can cause people of color to feel indignant or cynical about race relations.

The racial perception gap is further complicated by what authors Leonard Steinhorn and Barbara Diggs-Brown refer to as a "cycle of misunderstanding." They contend that a chain reaction of misunderstandings begins with the notion that discrimination is no longer a problem in America. The more whites disclaim the existence of discrimination, the more blacks and other minorities feel compelled to insist that discrimination still occurs. "To the white ear that makes black demands seem strident and aggressive, which then reinforces the white view that blacks are complaining," maintain Steinhorn and Diggs-Brown. Many end up believing that minorities simply exaggerate their experiences of racism, while others conclude that whites are in deep denial about racism's current realities.

Addressing the intricacies of the perception gap is proving to be a daunting challenge for Americans. Many believe that whites and minorities must candidly discuss their experiences and differences of opinion with each other to arrive at a fuller understanding of what racial justice requires. Others, however, maintain that patience and forbearance—not dialogue—will lead the nation to a less polarized perspective on race relations. *Race Relations: Opposing Viewpoints* examines the racial perception gap and related issues in the following chapters: What Is the State of Race Relations in America? Is Racism a Serious Problem? How Should Policymakers Respond to Minorities' Concerns? How Can Race Relations Be Improved? The viewpoints presented in this volume will give readers valuable insights on the complexities of race and ethnicity in today's America.

CHAPTER 1

What Is the State of Race Relations in America?

Chapter Preface

In June 1998, three white men beat black hitchhiker James Byrd Jr. until he was unable to move, chained his ankles to their truck's back bumper, and dragged him until his body was beheaded and torn into pieces. Most Americans were shocked by this grisly racial murder in Jasper, Texas. It brought back disturbing memories of the South prior to the 1960s civil rights movement—a time when African Americans were frequently terrorized by whites intent on subjugating blacks and keeping the races separate.

In some ways, the outpouring of sympathy following Byrd's death reveals how much race relations have progressed since the middle of the twentieth century. Commentator Deroy Murdock reports that the Texas town "united after this tragedy. . . . Both black and white ministers led Jasper's 8000 citizens in interracial rallies and joint prayer vigils." Jasper's local leaders condemned the hatred that had led to Byrd's murder, proclaiming "This is not Jasper." President Bill Clinton agreed, insisting that "this is not what this country is all about." Such heartfelt outcry against bigotry suggests, for many, that America is no longer characterized by the intolerance that so often defined its past.

Yet not everyone agrees that America has largely overcome racism. Columnist Carl Rowan argues that Byrd's murder "reflects the hatred of more people in this country than most Americans want to admit." Murders resulting from racial hatred are relatively rare today, but many analysts contend that such crimes are the most extreme form of a more widespread problem. They maintain that subtle forms of racism—from workplace discrimination and housing segregation to ethnic stereotypes and veiled doubts about minorities' intelligence—remain prevalent. "Only when we truly stand up against the day-to-day racial injustices can we say honestly of a grotesque murder, 'This is not my town. This is not America,'" declares Rowan.

The authors in the following chapter present further debate about the state of race relations between whites and blacks, as well as relations among various minority groups.

"The land where individuals would 'not be judged by the color of their skin but by the content of their character'. . . seems every day more a reality."

Racial Harmony Prevails

Deroy Murdock

Racial harmony largely prevails in today's America, argues Deroy Murdock in the following viewpoint. He contends that although bigotry still exists, the vast majority of Americans are tolerant and do not see race as a divisive and troublesome issue. An increase in black representatives chosen by white electorates, a marked decrease in anti-Semitism, and the growing number of interracial marriages all confirm America's racial amity. Murdock is a cable television news commentator and a senior fellow with the Atlas Economic Research Foundation.

As you read, consider the following questions:

1. According to Murdock, how did the citizens of Jasper, Texas, respond after the bigoted and brutal murder of James Byrd Jr.?
2. Of the seventy allegedly antiblack church arsons in the 1990s that were investigated by the Department of Justice and *USA Today*, how many were found to be motivated by racism?
3. How many minors "of a different race than one or both of their parents" were discovered by the U.S. Census in 1990?

Excerpted from "Everyday America's Racial Harmony," by Deroy Murdock, *The American Enterprise*, November/December 1998. Reprinted by permission of *The American Enterprise*, a national magazine of politics, business, and culture.

It's August 2, 1998, in New York's Central Park as radical black poet Amiri Baraka reads a poem to musical accompaniment. "Suppose you was so out, your murder was not a crime," says Baraka (formerly LeRoi Jones). "Suppose you are the usual suspect in any crime, even those committed against you?" Baraka then recites a string of racial epithets: "Shine, Woogie, Rug head, Spear chucker, coon, jigaboo. . . ."

In the back of the Summer Stage audience, a young white guy in a blue T-shirt strokes his chin and looks puzzled. And why not? Baraka heaps his avalanche of black victimology upon a friendly, well-integrated crowd of white, black, Hispanic, and Asian spectators. They cheerfully sway on a sun-splashed Sunday to the sounds of black American and African musicians. A blond woman dances with abandon behind a black baby's stroller.

The sunshine bounces off the gray chest hairs that upholster an older white man twirling beside several black patrons. Beneath a shady tree, a white woman laughs and chats in French with a half-dozen young African men as dark as the night is long. They seem to be old friends. Against these scenes of racial tranquillity, Baraka is on stage yelling: "liver lips, sambo, boy, Burr head, property, darkie, ink spot. . . ."

His words sound oddly alien to a country that quietly has eased racial tensions. While left-wing activists like the Reverends Jesse Jackson and Al Sharpton complain constantly about what they consider the white man's never-ending war against minorities, Americans of different ethnic backgrounds actually are making peace with each other. They're demonstrating quite clearly that, to paraphrase Rodney King, we all *can* just get along.

Playing Up the Bad News

But don't tell that to America's so-called "black leaders." They see a bigot under every bed. "Everywhere we see clear racial fault lines, which divide American society as much now as at anytime in our past," NAACP chairman Julian Bond declared in May 1998.

"Hardly an aspect of American life has escaped the baneful touch of this awful thing called racism," said historian John Hope Franklin, chairman of President Clinton's advisory

20

board on race, in July 1997. "Wherever you go, you are going to see this."

"We are the victims of racism in this society," Rep. Louis Stokes (D-Ohio) announced in June 1997.

Jim Sleeper, author of *Liberal Racism*, believes "there is a race industry that has a moral and financial stake in ginning up these racial bogeymen." As he says by phone: "There is a real effort to play up the bad news and play down the good. . . . The ground is shifting under our feet, and a lot of these people don't want to let go."

Neither Sleeper nor anyone else argues that bigotry is extinct. Those who think so need only consider the case of James Byrd, Jr. Words as ugly as those hurled by Amiri Baraka may have been the last things Byrd heard on June 7, 1998, when three white ex-convicts picked up the disabled 49-year-old black man as he hitchhiked. In an horrific crime that shocked and outraged Americans, they chained him to their pickup truck and dragged him to death by the ankles.

But this atrocity overshadowed the racial harmony that the people of Jasper, Texas, previously enjoyed, and soon worked diligently to restore. The town that many journalists dismissed as a bigoted backwater united after this tragedy. Jasper's black mayor, R.C. Horn, and both black and white ministers led Jasper's 8,000 citizens in interracial rallies and joint prayer vigils. With love and respect, they convened to protest the human tragedy that had befallen their neighbor. After one service, the mixed crowd hugged and sang "We Shall Overcome."

In a half-hearted attempt at healing, even a few members of the Ku Klux Klan showed up to "denounce what has happened." They explained that there were some things even *they* could not applaud. Hate without homicide seems like progress, of a sort. When the New Black Panther Party arrived to protest the June 27 Klan demonstration, most Jasper residents avoided both groups, and asked outsiders to leave them in peace.

Racial Reconciliation

Jasper's racial reconciliation mirrors that which occurred when the media diagnosed an epidemic of supposedly antiblack church fires that turned out to be far less incendiary. As journalist Michael Fumento explains, only three of over 70 church fires investigated by *USA Today* and the Department of Justice could be tied to racial animosity. The federal Church Arson Task Force likewise uncovered few racial links. Several burned black churches were struck by lightning. Others were torched for insurance money. Young vandals set still more ablaze. Many were burned by copy-cat arsonists fueled, ironically, by media condemnation of previous fires. One-third of those arrested were black.

Racial Attitudes Have Changed

Actually, white racial attitudes have so radically changed that today 87 percent of blacks say they have a white friend, while 86 percent of whites report having a black friend. It has become not the least bit unusual for blacks and whites to have brought someone of the other race home to dine, and most blacks and whites say their neighborhood is racially mixed.

The racial divide has certainly not disappeared; the O.J. Simpson trial was a sobering reminder of that fact. But the ground gained should not be ignored. Even in the most intimate of relations, there has been substantial change. By 1993, 12 percent of all marriages contracted by African Americans were to a white.

Abigail and Stephan Thernstrom, *San Diego Union-Tribune*, September 21, 1997.

Well before the "racist arson" theory was debunked, white churchgoers embraced the black faithful. The Christian Coalition established a $1 million Save the Churches Fund to help rebuild black houses of worship. Ralph Reed, the Christian Coalition's then-executive director, met with black ministers in June 1996. "We come not trying to preach to others," he said, but to learn from those who struggled "for racial justice, a cause which in the past the white evangelical church failed to embrace, to its great shame." What began as a wave of reputedly anti-black arson became a cause for bridge building between blacks and whites.

The January 16, 1997 death of Ennis Cosby—son of comedian Bill Cosby and his wife Camille—has been portrayed as a brutal bias crime that was inevitable in this hopelessly racist society. "I believe America taught our son's killer to hate African Americans," Mrs. Cosby wrote in *USA Today*. "Racism and prejudice are omnipresent and eternalized in America's institutions, media, and myriad entities."

Ennis Cosby's murder, however, looks like little more than a simple, vicious street crime, perpetrated by a Ukranian immigrant named Mikail Markhasev. While perhaps not an ethnic Eden, today's America mostly teaches tolerance to arrivals from other countries. Why did 40 percent of U.S. respondents recently select Bill Cosby as "the nation's top dad" if these really are the United States of Racism? Why does a racist Amerikkka buy Bill Cosby's hugely successful books, watch his TV shows, and buy the Jell-O Pudding Pops he endorses? Beyond the national outpouring of grief at her son's senseless death, Mrs. Cosby overlooks stark material proof of America's affection for her husband: a decades-long stream of big money. In 1997 alone, *Forbes* reports Cosby earned $18 million. This demonstrated public fondness underscores the folly of Camille Cosby's theory of innate American bigotry—unless one believes that people give money, by the vault-full, to those they hate.

For that matter, would white bigots vote for blacks? Whites increasingly choose blacks to represent them in office. New York State Comptroller Carl McCall, Ohio State Treasurer Kenneth Blackwell, Colorado Secretary of State Vikki Buckley, former U.S. Senator Carol Moseley-Braun of Illinois, and former Virginia Governor Douglas Wilder are examples of black Democrats and Republicans favored by heavily white electorates. . . .

America's Growing Racial Amity

Corroborating evidence of America's growing racial amity can be found in the dramatic decrease in anti-Semitism. The Anti-Defamation League reported an 8.8 percent drop in anti-Semitic vandalism and other crimes in 1997. As Irving Kristol has remarked: "the danger facing American Jews today is not that Christians want to persecute them, but that Christians want to marry them." According to the 1990 National Jewish Population Survey, 52 percent of American Jews intermarry with Gentiles.

Intermarriage exists among many groups. The 1990 Census found 1.4 million interracial married couples in America. In 1970, 0.7 percent of black women married white men; by 1993, that number had increased more than five-fold to 3.9 percent. Among black men in 1970, 1.9 percent married white women. That figure more than quadrupled to 8.9 percent in 1993.

The numbers are even higher among other ethnicities. As John J. Miller reports in his book, *The Unmaking of Americans*, in 1990, 28 percent of all marriages involving someone of Mexican ancestry also included a non-Hispanic. Half of Americans of Japanese descent marry people without Japanese roots. Miller observes that intermarriage among whites once was noteworthy. "When an Irish American married an Italian American 75 years ago," he writes, "it was probably a big deal in the neighborhood. But no more. In the future, everyone will have a Korean grandmother."

Of course, interracial couples most profoundly blur America's ethnic lines by having mixed children. The 1990 Census discovered 2 million minors who were "of a different race than one or both of their parents." This trend has grown so widespread that some multi-racial couples demanded a "mixed race" box on the 2000 Census form. After much deliberation, the Census Bureau instead decided to allow Americans to describe themselves by filling as many racial-category boxes as they wish.

Couples who adopt also find that race lines are drawn in chalk rather than ink, if at all. Despite the National Association of Black Social Workers' claim that trans-racial adoption is "cultural genocide," Congress easily passed the Multiethnic Placement Act in 1994. It prohibits racial discrimination in adoption, and blocks federal funds to social-service agencies that prevent interracial adoption. This measure was strengthened in 1996.

Martin Luther King's Dream

In June 1998, I accompanied a group of college students to the Martin Luther King Center in Atlanta. These white youths and I, a 34-year-old black man, were equally startled by the surreal Jim Crow laws on display at the Center. One ordinance required all circuses visiting Louisiana to maintain separate entrances for white and black spectators. Another demanded separate buildings for black and white residents at an institution for the blind.

That world might as well be Mars. Americans may never be as truly colorblind as the occupants of that home for the sightless, but in U.S. churches, TV studios, voting booths, and even bedrooms, one thing is becoming clear: The land where individuals would "not be judged by the color of their skin but by the content of their character"—as Dr. King put it—seems every day more a reality than a decades-old dream.

"Our professed attitudes, symbols, and public expressions masquerade as integrated when our lives clearly are not."

Racial Harmony Does Not Prevail

Leonard Steinhorn and Barbara Diggs-Brown

Leonard Steinhorn and Barbara Diggs-Brown are professors at American University's School of Communication and the authors of *By the Color of Our Skin: The Illusion of Integration and the Reality of Race.* In the following viewpoint, they contend that genuine racial harmony does not exist in America. While the majority of Americans condemn overt racism, whites tend to avoid integrating with blacks, moving away from neighborhoods and schools when they become populated by blacks. Moreover, the authors maintain, most whites believe that America's racial problems were solved during the civil rights movement of the 1960s, while most blacks see discrimination as a current and ongoing problem. Such differences of opinion between whites and blacks belie the vision of a racially congenial America.

As you read, consider the following questions:
1. What factors do liberals and conservatives believe led to today's racial problems, according to the authors?
2. According to Steinhorn and Diggs-Brown, how many whites and blacks attended Washington, DC's Roosevelt High School in 1963?
3. What do most whites believe is the source of problems for blacks, in the authors' opinion?

Excerpted from *By the Color of Our Skin*, by Leonard Steinhorn and Barbara Diggs-Brown. Copyright ©1999 by Leonard Steinhorn and Barbara Diggs-Brown. Used by permission of Dutton, a division of Penguin Putnam Inc.

There is a conventional wisdom about the 1960s that most writers and commentators follow. The story line is this: we came close, very close, to solving America's racial dilemma completely in the mid-sixties, until a number of factors stalled our progress and undermined the consensus. Great strides were made toward integration, according to this view, but unfortunately we now live with a bitter aftertaste. This version fits with the popular tendency to look at the early 1960s through the romance and nostalgia of Camelot and King, an innocent time when the great civil rights struggles united the black and white majority in America. We had a teachable moment for racial harmony, the story goes, and we squandered it. To liberals, blame for our current problems falls squarely on President Richard Nixon's parochial and cynical strategy to build a silent majority from racial resentment and to draw discontented George Wallace voters into the Republican party—the southern strategy. It was a strategy that, liberals say, Ronald Reagan turned into a fine art. To conservatives, the villains include the black nationalists who fueled racial discontent and the liberal social engineers who rationalized violent crime and foisted divisive policies like busing, affirmative action, and group rights on well-meaning middle-class whites, deeply embittering them. To be sure, this type of finger-pointing is as much about present agendas as past events, but this fact should not obscure the similarity between the liberal and conservative points of view: that we had a chance to put this racial thing behind us if people had only put the national interest ahead of their special interest.

A Separated America

The trouble is, this view is not wholly accurate. The fact that some of us dreamed of integrating does not mean it was ever close to happening. The civil rights movement ended legal segregation in America. It created unprecedented opportunities for black political power and economic mobility. It established a social norm that no longer tolerated or condoned overt discrimination and bigotry. It was no doubt a crowning moment in American history, justifiably embraced and celebrated today by people of every political stripe. But it simply

27

couldn't build an integrated America. As much as we like to blame the southern strategy, the silent majority, affirmative action, busing, race riots, multiculturalism, black power, or the precipitous rise of inner-city violent crime for poisoning the "beloved community," the evidence shows that the infrastructure of a separated America had already been established by the time any of these factors even entered the realm of race relations. The racially divided urban and suburban housing patterns of today were set in place in the early sixties. So were the dynamics around desegregated schooling. Even the way we now interact and perceive each other was foreshadowed then. In November 1964, only four months after Congress passed the 1964 Civil Rights Act outlawing discrimination in employment, government programs, and public accommodations—a law whose purpose, as President Lyndon Johnson stated, "is not to divide, but to end divisions"—the people of California, by a resounding two-to-one margin, approved a constitutional amendment for their state that overturned an open housing law and effectively allowed racial discrimination in housing. We may get misty-eyed when we think back to Martin Luther King's remarkable speech at the 1963 March on Washington, but barely two months later, Bower Hawthorne, the editor of two Minneapolis papers, the *Star* and *Tribune*, said, "We're getting increasing complaints from our readers that we are overplaying the integration story. Some of our white readers are getting tired of reading so much about it." We can accuse Nixon, Reagan, limousine liberals, black leaders, urban ethnics, or the social engineers of sowing discord, but they were merely acting out roles that in many ways already had been written for them in the early sixties. To those who decry what they see as the balkanization of America by racial preferences today, the truth is that the boundary lines of today's balkanization were shaped long before racial preferences even became an issue. To those who fret over what they see as resegregation today, the sad truth is that there was never an integration from which to resegregate. . . .

White Backlash

Many of these same [white backlashers] voted against real integration with their feet as early as the 1950s, and there was no shortage of overt backlash among self-proclaimed moderates even during the halcyon days of the civil rights era—before affirmative action, race riots, black power, and busing supposedly alienated them. Praise for the bedrock fairness of America's middle class is a staple of political rhetoric these days, but the bottom-line is this: from the very beginning of the civil rights movement, from the moment desegregation became the law of the land, most whites were willing to accept and indeed applaud a degree of public interaction with blacks, but drew the line when it came to family, home, social life, school, and work—the linchpins of real integration. Whenever and wherever blacks threatened to cross that line, whites first tried to flee and then, tired of running, resisted and fought. . . .

In October 1964, one of America's greatest political journalists looked into the crystal ball and wrote a prophetic, searing essay for *Life* magazine on white middle-class resistance to integration. Backlash, observed Theodore H. White, is "as invisible, yet as real, as air pollution." It would probably not show up in the 1964 presidential election results, he wrote, but it "is an unease whose impact will be felt not as much now as over the long range," particularly as whites see increasing black encroachment on their holy trinity of home, school, and work. For the Democrats, the long-term peril of a divided party is clear, he noted. The Republican party, "born in racial strife, [must] choose whether it abandons its tradition and becomes the white man's party or refreshes its tradition by designing a program of social harmony." And so he concluded: "Only one political certainty can be stated now which will outlast next month's election: If, at this time when the nation is so rich and strong, both parties ignore the need for constructive answers to the question 'What Do They Want?,' then disaster lies ahead—and backlash—the politics of chaos—will carry over, its snap growing in violence from 1964 to 1968 and all the elections beyond, until the question *is* answered. . . ."

Neighborhoods and Schools

Consider the many survey findings that herald the good news of white America's tolerance. A significant majority of whites say they would prefer to live in a mixed neighborhood, perhaps as mixed as half black, half white. But almost everywhere you look in every part of the country where more than a token number of blacks live, whites begin to flee from their communities the minute the first black family moves in. Often these are suburban communities where the new homeowners are middle-class or even affluent blacks. It is a classic case of the domino effect: each black family that moves in increases the likelihood that the remaining white families will leave. Integration exists only in the time span between the first black family moving in and the last white family moving out.

Reprinted by permission of Mickey Siporin.

The very era that we applaud for racial progress tells a different story in communities like Sherman Park near Milwaukee, which lost 61 percent of its whites between 1970 and 1990; or Palmer Park, near Washington, D.C., which went from being virtually all white in the 1960s to virtually all black today; or the middle-class Philadelphia suburb of Yeadon, which doubled its black population in the 1980s, going from one-third to two-thirds black, and saw a corresponding decline among whites. Real estate agents will tell you that prospective white buyers show no interest in moving to these neighborhoods. . . .

The story is no different when it comes to schools. A majority of whites support mixed public schools, but apparently not for their own children. A 1993 survey of whites from the Minneapolis suburbs found that two-thirds favored sending white suburban children to the predominantly black Minneapolis public schools as a way to increase integration, but only seven percent said they would send their own child. . . .

In Baltimore, every one of the nine all-white schools that were required to integrate in 1954 had become all-black just seven years later. Roosevelt High School in northwest Washington, D.C., had 747 whites and no blacks in 1953, the year before desegregation; 634 whites and 518 blacks in 1955, the second year of desegregation; and 19 whites and 1,319 blacks in 1963, the tenth year of desegregation. White parents in Milwaukee even protested when some black children were transferred temporarily to white schools in 1963 while schools in predominantly black neighborhoods were being rebuilt. Years before busing roiled the educational waters, the pattern of school separation had been set. . . . In community after community, the story is the same: blacks make up a significantly larger proportion of schoolchildren than their percentage of the school-age population, which means that large numbers of whites begin to flee the system for private schools when the black student population inches above the token. . . . As of 1998, there were fewer than 4,000 white children left in Atlanta's public schools. Nor should we be misled if the numbers for an entire school district make it appear integrated; the actual schools themselves are often segregated by race. In Illinois, Michigan, New York, and New Jersey, almost three in five black public school students attend schools that have fewer than 10 percent whites. . . .

The Integration Illusion

The dissonance between professed racial attitudes and actual racial reality should come as no surprise. Ever since the 1960s, as society began to shun overt bigotry and applaud gestures of racial tolerance, social scientists have found whites to exaggerate their contact with and support for blacks. As with any norm, people understandably want to be seen as conforming to it—in this case, they are evincing society's antiracist and tolerant attitudes. In exit polls after elections, for example, more whites say they vote for black candidates than actually do. One study compared the different responses offered when the phone survey interviewer could be clearly identified as white or black. On topics such as racially mixed schools, friendships with blacks, and who's to blame for current black problems, white survey respondents who were interviewed by blacks consistently provided a more liberal or integrationist response than whites who were interviewed by whites. . . .

The point here is not to deny the credibility of all polls, many of which can be useful in comparing black and white attitudes, but merely to show how powerfully the integration illusion defines our perceptions and self-image. Call it racial civility, decorous integration, or the politeness conspiracy—the bottom line is that our professed attitudes, symbols, and public expressions masquerade as integrated when our lives clearly are not. And what people say is less important than what they do. . . .

To be sure, let us not overlook an important area of consensus: blacks and whites share a nearly unanimous distaste for overt expressions of bigotry and blatant acts of discrimination. Considering the state of our nation just four decades ago, we should not underrate this accomplishment. We should be proud of establishing the norm and knowing it will not change. Beyond this, however, there is little consensus.

Whites' Views on Discrimination

Most compelling are the different ways whites and blacks view the problem of discrimination. According to surveys on race conducted over the years, a substantial proportion of whites say that the civil rights gains of the 1960s largely ended the problem of discrimination in America. Whites see themselves as well meaning and concerned about racial equality. They believe themselves to be fair, if not colorblind, and they cannot imagine themselves as blatantly discriminating. With Jim Crow gone and outright bigotry diminishing, most whites just don't see discrimination as a major barrier for blacks any longer. They think Dr. King's integration dream is within reach. "Large majorities think blacks now have the same opportunities as whites in their communities in terms of obtaining jobs, housing and education," the Gallup Poll News Service reported in 1989. "Many whites are unable to name even one type of discrimination that affects blacks in their area." As columnist William Raspberry observed in 1995, "Younger whites know the cruder facts: that America once had slavery and Jim Crow and now has Colin Powell. Their sense . . . is of a problem confronted and mostly resolved." The problem is so resolved, most whites believe, that society has gone too far to accommodate blacks. Significant majorities of whites tell pollsters that prejudice harms blacks much less than affirmative action harms whites. Whites are not oblivious to the problems discrimination can cause blacks, but if anyone is to blame for black problems today, whites point the finger at blacks. They simply don't have the willpower or motivation to improve their lot, whites believe. All of these views are not of recent mint . . . they actually began to form during the early civil rights days in the 1960s, before affirmative action and welfare became national issues. So it is safe to say that whites have a fairly static and consistent view of black life, which has developed over the past three decades: discrimination no longer unduly hobbles blacks, government has helped blacks at the expense of whites, and blacks have only themselves to blame for their problems. Given these assumptions, white opposition to affirmative action and other government programs seems logical. . . .

The Racial Perception Gap

The discrimination may be more subtle today, but blacks feel it just as deeply. It is expressed not in the blatant fifties style—"blacks need not apply"—but in the subtle cues and decisions that are made on a daily basis. Blacks also see how whites hear about jobs and opportunities—through their church, union, sports club, community group, or fraternity network—and they know they will never be part of that. So as blacks see it, they have made progress in spite of these obstacles, with little help from whites. Their dream of the integration of truly color-blind equals remains precisely that, a dream. Blacks don't deny they are partly at fault for their problems, but they see society changing much less than whites think it has changed, and they see whites growing indifferent to racial problems altogether. . . .

These different views of discrimination spill over into the larger perception gap about life and politics in America. Generally speaking, whites believe that our nation's problems with racism and civil rights were solved three decades ago, while blacks see racial discrimination as an ongoing and daily obstacle to opportunity and equality. When blacks see discrimination, whites see equal opportunity. When blacks say civil rights, whites say special interests. When blacks support affirmative action, whites label it quotas, preferential treatment, and reverse discrimination. And where blacks see racism, whites respond that they are being overly sensitive. . . .

Integration is an ideal both of us [authors] would prefer to see realized in our lifetimes. A truly color-blind, integrated America is a vision we share. We believe it is in the best interest of all Americans, black and white. Part of us wants to buy in to the integration illusion, to praise the emperor's clothes, to embrace the hope of the dreamers that yes, it can work. We want a happy ending. But try as we might, the facts simply fail to accommodate our desires, and the racial reality stubbornly refuses to change.

"*While anti-Semitism is generally on the wane in this country, it has been on the rise among black Americans.*"

Anti-Semitism Threatens Black-Jewish Relations

Henry Louis Gates Jr.

In the following viewpoint, Henry Louis Gates Jr. maintains that anti-Semitism is on the rise among young and educated African Americans. This anti-Jewish sentiment is fostered by misguided activists who believe that the black community will become stronger if it isolates itself from other ethnic groups—particularly those who have allied themselves with blacks in the past. The author contends that African Americans cannot ignore anti-Semitism in the black community if they hope to combat racial and social injustice. Gates is chair of the Department of Afro-American Studies at Harvard University.

As you read, consider the following questions:

1. In Gates's opinion, what is the "bible of the new anti-Semitism"?
2. According to the author, American Jewish merchants were accountable for what percentage of slave trafficking in the New World?
3. What happened at the black-Jewish forum that was held at the Church of St. Paul and Andrew in 1997, according to Gates?

Excerpted from "Black Demagogues and Pseudo-scholars," by Henry Louis Gates Jr., which appeared as an article on the Simon Wiesenthal Center's website at www.wiesenthal.com/resource/Blackdem.htm. Reprinted by permission of the author.

During the past decade, the historic relationship between African-Americans and Jewish Americans—a relationship that sponsored so many of the concrete advances of the civil rights era—showed another and less attractive face. While anti-Semitism is generally on the wane in this country, it has been on the rise among black Americans. A recent survey finds not only that blacks are twice as likely as whites to hold anti-Semitic views but—significantly—that it is among the younger and more educated blacks that anti-Semitism is most pronounced.

The New Anti-Semitism

The trend has been deeply disquieting for many black intellectuals. But it is something most of us, as if by unstated agreement, simply choose not to talk about. At a time when black America is beleaguered on all sides, there is a strong temptation simply to ignore the phenomenon or treat it as something strictly marginal. And yet to do so would be a serious mistake. As the African-American philosopher Cornel West has insisted, attention to black anti-Semitism is crucial, however discomfiting, in no small part because the moral credibility of our struggle against racism hangs in the balance. . . .

We must begin by recognizing what is new about the new anti-Semitism. Make no mistake: This is anti-Semitism from the top down, engineered and promoted by leaders who affect to be speaking for a larger resentment. This top-down anti-Semitism, in large part the province of the better educated classes, can thus be contrasted with the anti-Semitism from below common among African-American urban communities in the 1930's and 40's, which followed in many ways a familiar pattern of clientelistic hostility toward the neighborhood vendor or landlord.

In our cities, hostility of this sort is now commonly directed toward Korean shop owners. But "minority" traders and shopkeepers elsewhere in the world—such as the Indians of East Africa and the Chinese of Southeast Asia—have experienced similar ethnic antagonism. Anti-Jewish sentiment can also be traced to Christian anti-Semitism, given the historic importance of Christianity in the black community.

Unfortunately, the old paradigms will not serve to explain

the new bigotry and its role in black America. For one thing, its preferred currency is not the mumbled epithet or curse but the densely argued treatise; it belongs as much to the repertory of campus lecturers as community activists. And it comes in wildly different packages.

A book popular with some in the "Afro-centric" movement, *The Iceman Inheritance: Prehistoric Sources of Western Man's Racism, Sexism and Aggression*, by Michael Bradley, argues that white people are so vicious because they, unlike the rest of mankind, are descended from the brutish Neanderthals. More to the point, it speculates that the Jews may have been the "'purest,' and oldest Neanderthal-Caucasoids," the iciest of the ice people; hence (he explains) the singularly odious character of ancient Jewish culture. . . .

Sophisticated Hate Literature

The bible of the new anti-Semitism is *The Secret Relationship Between Blacks and Jews*, an official publication of the Nation of Islam that boasts 1,275 footnotes in the course of 334 pages.

Sober and scholarly looking, it may well be one of the most influential books published in the black community in the 1990s. It is available in black-oriented shops in cities across the nation, even those that specialize in Kente cloth and beads rather than books. It can also be ordered over the phone, by dialing 1-800-48-TRUTH. Meanwhile, the book's conclusions are, in many circles, increasingly treated as damning historical fact. The book, one of the most sophisticated instances of hate literature yet compiled, was prepared by the historical research department of the Nation of Islam. It charges that the Jews were "key operatives" in the historic crime of slavery, playing an "inordinate" and "disproportionate" role and "carving out for themselves a monumental culpability in slavery—and the black holocaust." Among significant sectors of the black community, this brief has become a credo of a new philosophy of black self-affirmation.

To be sure, the book massively misrepresents the historical record, largely through a process of cunningly selective quotation of often reputable sources. But its authors could be confident that few of its readers would go to the trouble of actually hunting down the works cited. For if readers actually did so, they might discover a rather different picture.

Reprinted by permission of Ann Telnaes.

They might find out—from the book's own vaunted authorities—that, for example, of all the African slaves imported into the New World, American Jewish merchants accounted for less than 2 percent, a finding sharply at odds with the Nation of Islam's claim of Jewish "predominance" in this traffic. They might find out that in the domestic trade it appears that all of the Jewish slave traders combined bought and sold fewer slaves than the single gentile firm of Franklin and Armfield. In short, they might learn what the historian Harold Brackman has documented—that the book's repeated insistence that the Jews dominated the slave trade depends on an unscrupulous distortion of the historic record. . . .

A Theology of Guilt

However shoddy the scholarship of works like *The Secret Relationship*, underlying it is something even more troubling: the tacit conviction that culpability is heritable. For it suggests a doctrine of racial continuity, in which the racial evil of a people is merely manifest (rather than constituted) by their historical misdeeds. The reported misdeeds are thus the signs of an essential nature that is evil.

How does this theology of guilt surface in our everyday moral discourse? In New York, in the spring of 1997, a forum was held at the Church of St. Paul and Andrew to provide an occasion for blacks and Jews to engage in dialogue on such issues as slavery and social injustice. Both Jewish and black panelists found common ground and common causes. But a tone-setting contingent of blacks in the audience took strong issue with the proceedings. Outraged, they demanded to know why the Jews, those historic malefactors, had not apologized to the "descendants of African kings and queens."

And so the organizer of the event, Melanie Kaye Kantrowitz, did. Her voice quavering with emotion, she said: "I think I speak for a lot of people in this room when I say 'I'm sorry.' We're ashamed of it, we hate it, and that's why we organized this event." Should the Melanie Kantrowitzes of the world, whose ancestors survived Czarist pogroms and, latterly, the Nazi Holocaust, be the primary object of our wrath? And what is yielded by this hateful sport of victimology, save the conversion of a tragic past into a game of recrimination? Perhaps that was on the mind of another audience member. "I don't want an apology," a dreadlocked woman told her angrily. "I want reparations. Forty acres and a mule, plus interest."

The Strategy of Ethnic Isolationism

These are times that try the spirit of liberal outreach. In fact, Louis Farrakhan, leader of the Nation of Islam, himself explained the real agenda behind his campaign, speaking before an audience of 15,000 at the University of Illinois in 1996. The purpose of *The Secret Relationship*, he said, was to "rearrange a relationship" that "has been detrimental to us."

"Rearrange" is a curiously elliptical term here: If a relation with another group has been detrimental, it only makes sense to sever it as quickly and unequivocally as possible. In short, by "rearrange," he means to convert a relation of friendship, alliance and uplift into one of enmity, distrust and hatred. But why target the Jews? Using the same historical methodology, after all, the researchers of the book could have produced a damning treatise on the involvement of left-handers in the "black holocaust." The answer requires us to go beyond the usual shibboleths about bigotry and view the matter, from the demagogues' perspective, strategically: as the bid of one black elite to supplant another. It requires us, in short, to see anti-Semitism as a weapon in the raging battle of who will speak for black America—those who have sought common cause with others or those who preach a barricaded withdrawal into racial authenticity. The strategy of these apostles of hate, I believe, is best understood as ethnic isolationism—they know that the more isolated black America becomes, the greater their power. And what's the most efficient way to begin to sever black America from its allies? Bash the Jews, these demagogues apparently calculate, and you're halfway there.

I myself think that an aphorist put his finger on something germane when he observed, "We can rarely bring ourselves to forgive those who have helped us." For sometimes it seems that the trajectory of black-Jewish relations is a protracted enactment of this paradox.

Many Jews are puzzled by the recrudescence of black anti-Semitism in view of the historic alliance. The brutal truth has escaped them: that the new anti-Semitism arises not in spite of the black-Jewish alliance but because of it. For precisely such transracial cooperation—epitomized by the historic partnership between blacks and Jews—is what poses the greatest threat to the isolationist movement.

In short, for the tacticians of the new anti-Semitism, the original sin of American Jews was their involvement—truly "inordinate," truly "disproportionate"—not in slavery, but in the front ranks of the civil rights struggle.

Empty Gestures of Black Unity

For decent and principled reasons, many black intellectuals are loath to criticize "oppositional" black leaders. Yet it has become apparent that to continue to maintain a comradely silence may be, in effect, to capitulate to the isolationist agenda, to betray our charge and trust. And, to be sure, many black writers, intellectuals and religious leaders have taken an unequivocal stand on this issue.

Cornel West aptly describes black anti-Semitism as "the bitter fruit of a profound self-destructive impulse, nurtured on the vines of hopelessness and concealed by empty gestures of black unity."

After years of conservative indifference, those political figures who acquiesced, by malign neglect, to the deepening crisis of black America should not feign surprise that we should prove so vulnerable to the demagogues' rousing messages of hate, their manipulation of the past and present.

Bigotry, as a tragic century has taught us, is an opportunistic infection, attacking most virulently when the body politic is in a weakened state. Yet neither should those who care about black America gloss over what cannot be condoned: That much respect we owe to ourselves. For surely it falls to all of us to recapture the basic insight that Dr. Martin Luther King so insistently expounded. "We are caught in an inescapable network of mutuality," he told us. "Whatever affects one directly affects all indirectly." How easy to forget this—and how vital to remember.

> *"Blacks and Jews offer an important model for interethnic cooperation for a very diverse society."*

Black-Jewish Relations Are Not Deteriorating

Clarence Page

Anti-Semitism is not on the increase among African Americans, Clarence Page maintains in the following viewpoint. Surveys reveal that a majority of blacks and Jews believe that the two groups should work together on civil rights issues; only a minority claim that black-Jewish relations are deteriorating. Although African Americans and Jews may have strong differences of opinion about certain issues—particularly the role of Nation of Islam leader Louis Farrakhan—they generally feel optimistic about black-Jewish relations. Page is a nationally syndicated columnist.

As you read, consider the following questions:

1. According to the survey cited by Page, what percentage of blacks claimed that black-Jewish relations improved from 1996 to 1997?
2. In what ways have blacks and Jews worked together in the past, according to the author?
3. In Page's opinion, how does interethnic cooperation begin?

Reprinted, with permission, from "Still Partners After All These Years," by Clarence Page, *Liberal Opinion Week*, May 18, 1998; © Tribune Media Services. All rights reserved.

It was the first-ever national poll on how blacks and Jews feel about each other and it was keeping Rabbi Marc Schneier awake.

Schneier, president of the Foundation for Ethnic Understanding and of the New York Board of Rabbis, was troubled by a single thought:

What if he was wrong?

Have Black-Jewish Relations Deteriorated?

Schneier is one of many optimists who has been insisting for years that reports of deteriorating relations between blacks and Jews were greatly exaggerated. African-Americans and American Jews have their differences, like any groups, the rabbi has said. But, on the whole, he maintained the two groups continue to agree more than they disagree.

Now, for the first time, a major pollster, Kieran Mahoney of Kieran Mahoney & Associates, was conducting a national poll to see what most African-Americans and American Jews of all ages really think of each other.

The night before Schneier learned the results of the poll, which was released April 27, 1998, he was awakened in a cold sweat by the chilling possibility the poll might produce results other than those he hoped to see. The press conference already was scheduled. White and black dignitaries, including Martin Luther King III, were scheduled to appear.

What if the polls showed relations between blacks and Jews had collapsed? What kind of positive spin could he put on that?

Most Blacks and Jews Want a Partnership

Happily, no spin was necessary. As expected, the poll showed sharp differences on issues of racial "quotas" and Nation of Islam Minister Louis Farrakhan, whose highly critical statements regarding Jews, Judaism and Israel have drawn charges of anti-Semitism.

But the survey of 500 Jews and 500 African-Americans across the country also found that 69 percent of Jews and 59 percent of blacks thought blacks and Jews "should form a partnership to work on civil rights issues."

It also found 43 percent of Jews and 54 percent of blacks

Many Blacks Oppose Anti-Semitism

Great Black, heroic freedom fighters have been strong critics of anti-Semitism. W.E.B. Du Bois, Frederick Douglass, Martin King, Ella Baker, Malcolm X after Mecca, and many other leaders throughout our history have a legacy that needs to be built upon—people who were critical of anti-Semitism. The major weight of the Black Freedom Movement has been against anti-Semitism—so it's not just Cornel West or Henry Louis Gates or bell hooks who are critical of anti-Semitism—no. We're just echoing a richer tradition that came before us. When this history is made more explicit, more Blacks will understand that to engage in anti-Semitic rhetoric or actions runs counter to one of the important trends within our own history.

Michael Lerner and Cornel West, *Jews and Blacks: Let the Healing Begin*, 1995.

thought relations between the two groups had gotten better over the past year. Only 17 percent of Jews and 14 percent of blacks thought relations had gotten worse.

Significantly, Jews who had the highest "unfavorables" toward Farrakhan also showed the highest feelings that relations were deteriorating, Mahoney said afterward. "That was the only place among the figures where we got that kind of correlation, which indicates to me that Farrakhan is a key point of tension," he said.

Farrakhan drew "favorable" ratings of 19 percent from Jews and 49 percent from blacks and "unfavorable" ratings of 61.2 percent from Jews and 27 percent from blacks.

By contrast, Jesse Jackson received an 84 percent favorable rating from blacks and 54 percent from Jews.

The Attitudes of the Young

Unfortunately, the poll skirted over one important area that begs for further inquiry: the attitudes of the young.

As an African-American who came of age in the 1960s, I have detected less optimism and understanding among blacks and Jews who are too young to remember those happier times of coalition. Mahoney agreed. Younger respondents were "more negative and less inclined to believe relations are improving," he said, although they, too, were more inclined to say relations were getting better than worse.

One hopes their optimism will be rewarded. Like their elders, they will have to work at it.

Historically, blacks and Jews worked closely together in organized labor, the civil rights movement and various other causes. Today a new partnership of sorts is appearing in the private sector. An April 22, 1998, headline in the *Wall Street Journal* offers an example: "As Blacks Rise High in the Executive Suite, CEO is Often Jewish."

The Page One article by reporter Jonathan Kaufman, author of "Broken Alliance," a 1988 book about black-Jewish relations, describes top Jewish executives, like Michael Eisner at Walt Disney Co., Harvey Golub at American Express and Gerald Levin at Time Warner Inc., who have mentored the advancement of top black executives.

"It's more than coincidence," one black executive told Kaufman. "If you blaze the trail yourself, you are going to be more courageous in bringing someone else along."

In that way, blacks and Jews offer an important model for interethnic cooperation for a very diverse society. It begins with a refusal to allow the few people or issues that divide us to get in the way of the many concerns we have in common.

"Immigration has resulted in lost job opportunities for blacks, particularly in construction and manufacturing."

Blacks Are Losing Jobs to Immigrants

Joseph Daleiden

An increase in immigration has resulted in job loss for African Americans, argues Joseph Daleiden in the following viewpoint. In construction, for example, black contractors who pay eight to ten dollars an hour are losing out to contractors who hire immigrants at lower wages. Blacks also have difficulty finding work in many other fields, because employers often fulfill affirmative action requirements by hiring noncitizen immigrant minorities instead of African Americans. Daleiden, an author, economist, and demographer, is the president of the National Grassroots Alliance, an immigration-reform advocacy group.

As you read, consider the following questions:

1. Currently, how many legal and illegal immigrants come to the United States annually, according to Daleiden?
2. According to the author, blacks make up what percentage of employees in Korean-owned stores in New York City?
3. In Daleiden's view, why did black employment increase in Alabama, Arkansas, and Louisiana during the 1990–91 recession?

Reprinted from "Immigration's Impact on African-American Job Opportunities," by Joseph Daleiden, *Headway*, February 1998, by permission of Richberg Communications, Inc.

F requently politicians and the media try to frame the immigration debate in terms of whether or not the United States should continue immigration. Put that way, the answer seems self-evident. Few Americans wish to halt all immigration. However, the real issue regarding immigration today is the same as it always has been: how many immigrants should be permitted.

Throughout our history the number of immigrants has fluctuated from about 14,000 annually during the first 60 years of our republic to today's record high of 1,000,000 legal and between 300,000 to 500,000 illegal immigrants a year. To put today's immigration in perspective, the average number of immigrants since our nation's founding has been about 250,000 annually.

Immigration's Effect on Wages

Many of the studies examining the consequences of immigration focus on the aggregate impact on the economy. However, such aggregates frequently obscure how immigration affects various socioeconomic groups. The conclusion from a review of immigration studies, including the most recent study by the National Academy of Science (NAS) is that in general investors have benefited while many wage earners have suffered. This is not surprising, since basic economic theory tells us that whenever the supply of labor increases faster than demand real wage rates will decline. This has been the situation in the U.S. for the last 25 years. After adjusting for inflation, the average weekly earnings declined 19 percent between 1973 and 1996.

The decline in wages is due to more than just the increase in immigration. Greater international competition, increased mechanization, and the influx of the baby boom in the work force have all had substantial impacts. Nevertheless, immigration has played a major role in depressing earnings in professional occupations (particularly for college teachers, scientists, mathematicians, and physicians) and even more so for entry-level jobs. The NAS study concluded that 44 percent of the decline in real wages of high school dropouts from 1980 to 1995 was due to immigrants competing for entry-level jobs.

The high level of immigration in recent years has even negatively impacted immigrants themselves. Roughly 20 percent of immigrants are highly skilled and educated; they make out quite well. However, 80 percent of immigrants tend to be low skilled and poorly educated; they have not done well. For instance, despite all of the efforts to unionize farm workers and put pressure on growers through boycotts and strikes, the annual earnings of farm workers have declined 20 to 30 percent over the past 20 years. The reason is simple: the constant supply of new immigrant farm workers continues to outstrip demand. In California today there are approximately two farm workers for every job.

Black Communities Have Been Hard Hit

America's black communities have also been particularly hard hit by excessive immigration. Most persons do not realize that the fastest increase in earnings for African-Americans occurred during the period 1940 through 1960, before affirmative action programs were introduced. The reason is that during most of this period there was a shortage of workers, and millions of blacks migrated from the South to get good paying jobs in northern factories.

However, during the last 20 years, many of these jobs have left the country for cheaper labor abroad. Other factory owners find that they can recruit lower cost Latino labor from Texas and California rather than turn to the inner city for employees. A recent analysis of labor force trends in the Midwest by race and occupation indicates that immigration has resulted in lost job opportunities for blacks, particularly in construction and manufacturing. During the 1990–91 recession, blacks lost far more jobs in these two industries than Hispanics, and blacks added far fewer jobs during the recovery.

In construction, black contractors have seen a steady erosion of jobs because their pay scales of $8 to $10 an hour cannot compete with contractors hiring immigrant labor for minimum wage. In manufacturing, which employs five times as many workers as construction, Hispanics almost doubled their share of jobs while the blacks' share declined significantly. In 1983, blacks held 280,000 more manufacturing jobs than Hispanics. But while Hispanics added 139,000 jobs between 1983 and 1995, black employment grew by only about 5,000 jobs.

The Future of Black Employment

Of particular concern for the future of black employment in the Midwest—as in other areas of the country—is that in terms of the rate of growth, Hispanics are outpacing blacks in every major occupation group. This should not be surprising since the growth rate of the Hispanic population in the Midwest is far higher than that of blacks.

Between 1980 and 1995 the black population grew only 16.1 percent while the number of Hispanics soared 63.5 percent. As Hispanics gain fluency in English, we may find trends similar to construction and manufacturing, i.e., during recessions blacks are first to be laid off and last to be rehired.

To make matters worse, as a result of expanding affirmative action programs to other minority groups such as Asian and Hispanic, employers can now effectively discriminate against African-Americans by hiring non-citizen immigrant minorities. While such an action violates the 1964 Civil Rights Act, it is widely practiced since the Equal Employment Opportunity Commission (EEOC) has rarely, if ever, prosecuted a minority employer for discriminating against blacks, nor have they prosecuted any employer for discriminating against blacks in favor of another minority.

A New Pattern of Discrimination

The result of the way affirmative action is administered has resulted in a new insidious pattern of discrimination. Consider the following:

• In New York, whose population is 25 percent black, only 5 percent of the employees who work in Korean-owned stores are African-American, while more than one-third are Mexican and Latin American immigrants. Even in Harlem, the percentage of Hispanic employees outnumbers blacks. (By the way, it isn't true that blacks will not accept low-paying jobs, as often alleged—it is estimated that in Harlem there are 14 job applicants for every minimum wage job.)

• In Los Angeles, which is 17 percent black, only 2 percent of small Korean-owned businesses hire blacks.

Tensions Between Blacks and Hispanics

For African Americans at the bottom [of the job market], research indicates that immigration, particularly of Latinos with limited education, has increased joblessness and frustration.

In Miami, where Cuban immigrants dominate the political landscape, tensions are high between Hispanics and blacks, says Nathaniel J. Wilcox, a community activist there. "The perception in the black community, the reality, is that Hispanics don't want some of the power, they want all the power," Wilcox says. "At least when we were going through this with the whites during the Jim Crow era, at least they'd hire us. But Hispanics won't allow African Americans to even compete. They have this feeling that their community is the only community that counts."

William Booth, *Washington Post National Weekly Edition*, March 2, 1998.

• Nationwide, one-half of the Small Business Administration set aside contracts go to firms owned by immigrants or children of immigrants.

• In California during the 1980s, the employment of African-Americans as bank tellers fell 39 percent while jobs for foreign-born tellers increased by 56 percent. Similar displacement has been found among janitors, hotel maids, waiters, and hospital nursing assistants and orderlies.

• A study of EEOC records of large firms revealed that during the 1990–91 recession, Asians and Hispanics gained 55,104 and 60,040 jobs, respectively, while blacks lost 59,479 jobs. In almost every state blacks lost jobs. Ironically, only in Alabama, Arkansas and Louisiana—states most noted for past discrimination against blacks—did the employment of blacks increase significantly. The reason is that there has been a minimal amount of immigration into these states.

History has a way of repeating itself, with often tragic consequences. Prior to the great wave of immigration at the turn of the twentieth century, blacks were moving up the economic ladder, getting jobs in the various trades. But with the huge influx of immigrants, black job opportunities quickly dried up. Leaders such as Frederick Douglass and Booker T. Washington objected to a trend that they knew would be devastating to their people. Douglass wrote, "Every hour sees the black man elbowed out of employment by some newly arrived immigrant whose hunger and whose color are thought to give him a better title to the place."

It is at least arguable that had America employed its black population at the turn of the twentieth century, black Americans would be far better off socially and economically than they are today. Additionally, all Americans would have benefited enormously by avoiding the billions of dollars expended trying to use welfare and affirmative action to solve a problem that a market economy would have resolved two generations ago. The answer is a job eligibility verification system to prevent employers from hiring illegal immigrants, and a reduction of legal immigration to the historic level of 250,000 annually.

"The impact [of immigration on African Americans] is tiny both in terms of job loss and decline in wages."

Blacks and Immigrants Need Honest Dialogue About Jobs

Elizabeth Martinez

Contrary to the conclusions of some analysts, immigration is not causing a significant rate of job loss among black Americans, contends Elizabeth Martinez in the following viewpoint. However, in cities with high immigration rates, it often looks as if immigrants are replacing blacks in service jobs—and this perception creates tension between African Americans and immigrants of color. This tension, Martinez argues, has been highlighted in a way that increases anti-immigrant sentiments. She maintains that blacks, Latinos, and Asians must join forces to counteract racist attitudes and win more jobs for all people. Martinez, author of *500 Years of Chicano History*, teaches women's studies at California State University in Hayward.

As you read, consider the following questions:
1. In what instances has immigration actually created jobs for African Americans, according to Martinez?
2. During the campaign for Proposition 187 in California, how did conservative organizations help fuel anti-immigrant sentiments among black citizens, according to the author?
3. According to Martinez, how have black and Latino advocacy groups worked together to fight racial and anti-immigrant discrimination?

Excerpted from "It's a Terrorist War on Immigrants," by Elizabeth Martinez, *Z Magazine*, July/August 1997. Reprinted with permission.

In the spring of 1997, a Latino immigrant who had worked legally in the United States for 40 years committed suicide after receiving a letter saying that under the new welfare law his Supplemental Security Income (SSI) might end. Not long afterward a wheelchair-bound Russian immigrant threw himself off his balcony from the same fear. Does this not suggest a monstrous assault that we must call terrorist?

What we once called "immigrant bashing" should be called immigrant smashing. It's an outright war, waged at the highest levels of government, as immigrant rights leader Maria Jimenez of Houston has long said. The war cabinet includes what we could call a Department of Propaganda, its purpose being to convince the public that some overwhelmingly poor, exploited, and vulnerable people are the enemy. Like many wars, this one utilizes vicious divide-and-conquer tactics to prevent a united resistance: divide Latinos, Asians, and the U.S.-born; the "undocumented" and the "documented"; recent and established arrivals. . . .

Job and Wage Competition

The vast majority of immigrants are people of color, for whom racism is the daily diet served along with immigrant status. Thus a potential for coalitions exists in Black communities. Alongside the commonality of racial oppression we also have the commonality of displacement—in the past or present—resulting from economic forces. But strong disunity has developed. Although often cultivated by divide-and-conquer tacticians, it must be taken seriously. We cannot ignore the issues of job and wage competition, with particular reference to Latinos and Blacks.

For several years, African American communities have believed that immigrants—meaning Latinos and Asians—are taking away jobs once available to Blacks. Defenders of immigrant rights have sometimes made the mistake of dismissing this concern arbitrarily. African American scholars cite such evidence as a 1993 *Wall Street Journal* study of the impact of the last recession which found that Blacks had lost 59,479 jobs across the U.S. (while other groups had a net gain) and that the worst losses were in states with the highest immigration rate, like Florida and California. Further, wages had gone down for

Blacks in some sectors where unionized Black workers once prevailed. Localized studies also encourage the sense of loss. For example, a study of the garment and hotel industries in New York City in 1940–90 found that immigrants' share of employment grew as the share of natives' employment fell.

Other scholars, usually white, have maintained that a very small amount of absolute job loss for African Americans may indeed occur in a few sectors. However, they say, immigration generates new jobs, which are then available to all. For example, in a particular city immigration may cause an increase in jobs at government agencies that offer services used by immigrants. Often African Americans, and rarely immigrants, are hired for such work. In other words, one must look at the total employment picture.

A Low Rate of Job Loss

A massive study by the National Research Council, released in draft form on May 17, 1997, agrees that there can be job loss, usually for less-skilled native workers, who compete with migrant workers—also less-skilled. This loss therefore affects primarily African Americans (but also low-income native Latinos). In other words, job loss does occur where the two categories of workers are similar in skill levels.

At the same time, states the 1997 report, the impact is tiny both in terms of job loss and decline in wages. Research on the job and wage loss for Black workers shows a negative impact of less than 1 percent for Blacks in general and even a tiny gain of +.02 for African American men (no data for women).

The study gives as a major reason for the low rate of job loss the fact that African Americans and immigrants usually live in different parts of the country. According to the report, 63 percent of African Americans live in states other than the six top immigration states (California, Florida, Illinois, New Jersey, New York, and Texas). In the 44 other states where most Blacks live, only 4 percent of the population are immigrants. But the evidence presented for this seems inadequate. How to explain Los Angeles and New York, where both African Americans and immigrants live in great numbers? In California as a whole, perhaps the weight of Los Angeles is offset by the Central Valley and northern

California which are largely white. As a result, on a statewide basis the report's explanation for low rates of African American job and wage loss may work statistically. The same might hold true on a nationwide basis, statistically.

The Impact of Human Perception

But there is another factor in Black anti-immigrant attitudes: people's perceptions. Rarely if ever do reports and statistics examine the impact of human perception on the debate about job loss. In evaluating how serious such loss is for African Americans, we cannot ignore reality as seen by a people for whom centuries of enslavement and the worst kind of brutalization will almost inevitably condition their perspective. When an African American goes to a hotel in the East where the service workers have always been Black and sees mostly Latino faces, the impact is powerful. The word spreads. Even if only a few jobs are involved—and poor jobs at that—the visual reality strikes home. "Don't tell me immigrants aren't taking jobs from Blacks," they might say. (Similarly, a Latino might go to a gas station in San Francisco's Mission District and find the gas station workers, once Latino, are now Asian.)

It is true, as the 1997 National Academy of Sciences report says, that immigrants represent only about 8 percent of the population, and so losses for any native group would have to be statistically huge to appear significant. Again, this fact doesn't undermine the psychological effect on communities that have been under racist and classist siege for centuries. That effect is aggravated, in the case of African Americans, by the fact that they will soon become the second largest U.S. population of color—no longer the first—if current immigration rates continue.

Job and wage competition as an issue has to be faced. We must do so with honest dialogue and a commitment to creating understanding—not more divisiveness. In the end, the question is not whether job loss really happens or not, and how much. The question is: do we let it divide African Americans and migrant workers, or do we acknowledge the problem, join forces to offset division, and work to win more jobs for everyone?

The Fostering of Racial Divisions

In answering that question, we all need to recognize how effectively division has been fostered, deliberately in some cases and out of ignorance in others. During the campaign for Prop. 187, the right-wing Federation for American Immigration Reform (FAIR) ran radio spots in Black communities that blamed their problems on those foreign hordes coming across the border. An anti-Asian commercial appeared on TV in which an African American car salesperson says, "Go see *Rising Sun* (the movie), then you'll know why you have to buy your car from me." The target was, of course, Japanese manufacturers but the ad encouraged racist attitudes toward all Asians. The passage of Prop. 187 in California, with a large Black vote in favor, was facilitated by such propaganda. [Proposition 187, which denied illegal immigrants certain public services, was overturned in 1998.]

Scapegoating Immigrants

The existence of job competition between Latino immigrants and African Americans (and possibly other U.S.-born minorities and more established immigrants) has been seized by some as a rationale for stopping immigration. This position—that immigrants hurt Blacks and the poor—is at best incomplete. In part, there is evidence that some types of immigration can be beneficial. To generalize about all immigration is an exercise in misleading polemics. Furthermore, to truly fight for Black equality in this country, a sound policy must include efforts to eradicate endemic racism. To focus only on immigrants as the source disadvantaging African Americans would, in our opinion, constitute scapegoating an already vulnerable group and miss the point. . . . Other factors, such as labor market discrimination and segmentation, are more important in explaining African American inequality. Even worse, focusing solely on immigration brings out a form of nativism that ultimately reinforces racially based prejudices.

Paul Ong and Abel Valenzuela Jr., *Ethnic Los Angeles*, 1996.

On the Latino or Asian/Pacific side, negative reactions to Black attitudes toward immigrants should also be discussed. Latinos know all too well that migrant workers have suffered greatly and even lost their lives by trying to come to this country. So it did hurt when the National Association for the Advancement of Colored People (NAACP) initially refused to take a position against employer sanctions. Imposed by the 1986 Immigration Reform and Control Act (IRCA), these sanctions were supposed to penalize employers for hiring undocumented workers. As a study by the U.S. General Accounting Office showed, their main effect has been discrimination against job-seekers based on appearance or accent, with many victims being citizens. In other words, racism.

The Black Congressional Caucus opposed sanctions early on, but the NAACP supported sanctions for a decade until Latino civil rights organizations threatened to resign from the National Civil Rights Leadership Conference. Finally the NAACP joined the opposition to sanctions. What should count here, from a Black/brown coalition-building perspective, is the NAACP's eventual support. Latinos and Blacks should also recall that the NAACP once worked together with LULAC (the League of Latin American Citizens) against segregation in the South at a time of intense Klan activity. Other examples of cooperation between the two peoples are described by several Black and brown scholars in Prof. Ishmael Reed's revealing 1997 anthology of essays by authors of all colors, *Multiamerica*.

The Need for Black-Latino Cooperation

Another real issue that comes up in relation to Black-Latino views of immigration is language. Too often in a workplace we can hear the question from an African American employee, "Why don't you speak English? You're in America now!" Again, it can help to understand that being denied the right to speak Spanish is an old form of racism which has plagued Latinos for decades. To speak Spanish represents defense of one's culture in a eurocentric, racist nation that doesn't want to remember Spanish—not English—was the common language in much of the Southwest for 250 years. (We can also note that some of the worst racist stereotypes about Asians are based on a hateful mockery of speech like "tickee" and "laundree" that homogenizes everything Asian as Chinese.) At the same time, other peoples facing racism— such as African Americans—may feel excluded by the use in their presence of a language they don't know. Sensitivity to these feelings is needed too.

All this touches only the tip of the iceberg. Relations between African Americans and Latinos (or other peoples of color) around immigration can be problematic in areas beyond work and culture. They come up in other aspects of urban life: neighborhoods changing, housing, equitable political representation, gangs. Whatever the arena of conflict, the goal needs to be greater cooperation and solidarity in opposing common enemies. Black Americans have sometimes called for such unity, like Joe Williams III, an African American writing in the *Los Angeles Sentinel* on September 9, 1996. Williams compared the current attacks on the undocumented to the harassment of Blacks during the 1950s–60s when many moved north or west as southern agriculture declined. "They were accused of taking the jobs of the white man. They were accused [by whites] of undermining the salaries of union workers." It's even worse today, Williams concluded, because mainstream Black politicians as well as segments of the Black and Latino communities join the attacks.

We need Latino voices like Williams's, people who will offer honest self-criticism about our attitudes toward African American concerns. We need more Latinos condemning the racist attitudes toward Blacks often found in our communities, along with African Americans coming to understand the Latino perspective and our commonalities. This kind of openness will take courage on both sides, not to mention all the other colors that must also communicate.

Periodical Bibliography

The following articles have been selected to supplement the diverse views presented in this chapter. Addresses are provided for periodicals not indexed in the *Readers' Guide to Periodical Literature*, the *Alternative Press Index*, the *Social Sciences Index*, or the *Index to Legal Periodicals and Books*.

American Enterprise	Section on race in America, November/December 1998.
William Booth	"Diversity and Division," *Washington Post National Weekly Edition*, March 2, 1998. Available from 1150 15th St. NW, Washington, DC 20071.
Richard Cohen	"America Looks Different to Minorities than It Does to Whites," *Liberal Opinion Week*, July 27, 1998. Available from 108 E. Fifth St., Vinton, IA 52349.
Ellis Cose	"Our New Look: The Colors of Race," *Newsweek*, January 1, 2000.
Mike Davis and Alessandra Moctezuma	"Policing the Third Border," *Colorlines*, Fall 1999.
Samuel Francis	"Diversity Leads to Conflict, Not Harmony," *Conservative Chronicle*, April 22, 1998. Available from PO Box 37077, Boone, IA 50037-0077.
Sarah E. Hinlicky	"Don't Write About Race," *First Things*, December 1999. Available from 156 Fifth Ave., Suite 400, New York, NY 10010.
Edwin D. Hoffman	"Being White in Black/White Relations: A Professor's Singular Life Journey," *Monthly Review*, March 1998.
John Kennedy Jr. and Louis Farrakhan	"One in a Million," *George*, October 1996. Available from 1633 Broadway, 41st Floor, New York, NY 10019.
Salim Muwakkil	"Letting Go of the Dream: African Americans Turn Their Backs on Integration," *In These Times*, November 2, 1997.
Poverty & Race	Section entitled "Is Integration Possible?" November/December 1999. Available from 3000 Connecticut Ave. NW, Suite 200, Washington, DC 20008.
Roberto Suro	"Strangers Among Us: How Latino Immigration Is Transforming America," *Hispanic*, July/August 1998. Available from 98 San Jacinto Blvd., Suite 1150, Austin, TX 78701.
Tim Wise	"Blinded by the White," *Z Magazine*, June 1999.

CHAPTER 2

Is Racism a Serious Problem?

Chapter Preface

Black dentist Elmo Randolph was pulled over by police on the New Jersey turnpike more than fifty times between 1991 and 1999. He was never given a ticket or cited for erratic driving. Instead, Randolph reports, an officer would approach his BMW, request his license and registration, and ask if he had any drugs or weapons in the car. Randolph contends that the only reason he has been stopped so often is because police are suspicious when they see a black man driving an expensive car: "Would they pull over a white middle-class person and ask the same question?"

Many maintain that police officers stereotype minorities as prone to criminal behavior and therefore they disproportionately stop and search blacks and Latinos. Statistics lend support to these charges. According to the New Jersey attorney general, 77 percent of the drivers stopped and searched by state police are black or Hispanic, but only 13.5 percent of motorists on the state's highways are black or Hispanic. Critics maintain that such "racial profiling"—the use of race as a factor in identifying potential suspects—humiliates and frightens law-abiding minorities. The possibility that police readily pursue individuals because of their color also increases concerns about unequal applications of the law and police harassment and abuse of minorities.

Others, however, argue that police target minorities simply because they have a higher incidence of criminal activity than whites do. According to *U.S. News & World Report*, blacks make up only 13 percent of the U.S. population but "make up 35 percent of all drug arrests and 55 percent of all drug convictions." If relatively high percentages of minorities are committing crimes, analysts point out, police should not be accused of undue bias when they pursue people of color as possible criminal suspects.

This dispute about the prevalence of bias among police is just one facet of today's controversy about racism in America. The authors in the following chapter probe the question of whether racism continues to place serious restrictions on minority rights and opportunities.

"[In white America], the images of blacks as less capable run strongly just beneath the surface of polite behavior."

White Racism Harms Blacks

David K. Shipler

David K. Shipler, a former *New York Times* correspondent, is the author of *A Country of Strangers: Blacks and Whites in America*. In the following viewpoint, he argues that the racist attitudes of whites continue to thwart life opportunities for blacks. Although today's racism is rarely blatant, antiblack prejudice still influences the opinions and behavior of many whites, leading to subtle instances of discrimination against blacks. Remedies such as affirmative action and diversity training, Shipler maintains, are still needed to address today's less obvious forms of racial bias.

As you read, consider the following questions:

1. According to the 1990 National Opinion Research survey cited by Shipler, what percentage of the population labeled blacks as "lazier than whites"?
2. What kinds of subtle discrimination can blacks face in seemingly integrated institutions, according to the author?
3. In what ways can negative stereotypes about blacks boost whites' self-esteem, in Shipler's opinion?

Reprinted from "Subtle vs. Overt Racism," by David K. Shipler, *The Washington Spectator*, March 15, 1998, by permission of *The Washington Spectator*; for a subscription, send a check for $15 to Public Concern Foundation, PO Box 20065, London Terrace Station, New York, NY 10011.

In Washington recently, after a panel discussion on race, a black attorney approached me with the following story. He had just headed a project for a federal agency. Midway through the work, one of his subordinates, a white woman, had confided to several other whites that she could not bear to take orders from a black person.

The whites, one of whom had been regarded by the black attorney as a friend, said nothing to him about her remark. Not until months later, toward the end of the project, did the friend finally inform him of the white woman's bias, and he then realized that the woman had been quietly sabotaging the work. The Federal agency dismissed her.

Prejudice Has Gone Underground

Incidents like this pockmark the surface of America, but they're rarely visible. Usually, whites camouflage their prejudices more deftly and are seldom fired for them. Here, however, the contradictory contours of the country's racial landscape were in plain view. On the one hand, a black man had risen to be the boss, and the white woman lost her job for acting out her bigotry—testimony to the anti-racism that has evolved since the civil rights movement.

But hidden roots of racial prejudice and tension were revealed: The white woman said what many whites feel but do not say—that blacks in authority make them uncomfortable. And many whites, like the black attorney's friend, are paralyzed into silence by others' expressions of racism. Where was the white friend's loyalty to the black boss? Had the friendship survived? I asked the black man. "We're working on it," he said.

The United States now finds itself in an era of race relations more complex than in the days of legal segregation. Bigotry then was blatant, so entrenched that it could be shattered ultimately only by the conscience of the country and the hammer of the law. Today, when explicit discrimination is prohibited and blatant racism is no longer fashionable in most circles, much prejudice has gone underground. It may have diminished in some quarters, but it is far from extinct. Like a virus searching for a congenial host, it mutates until it finds expression in a belief, a statement, or a form of behavior that seems acceptable.

The camouflage around such racism does not make it benign. It can still damage life opportunities. Take the durable, potent stereotype of blacks as unintelligent and lazy. In 1990, when the National Opinion Research Center at the University of Chicago asked a representative sample of Americans to evaluate various racial and ethnic groups, blacks ended up at the bottom. Most of those surveyed across the country labeled blacks as less intelligent than whites (53 percent); lazier than whites (62 percent); and more likely than whites to prefer being on welfare than being self-supporting (78 percent).

Stereotypes Contaminate Behavior

Much of this prejudice is no more than a thought, of course. To inhibit the translation of biased thoughts into discriminatory actions, American society has built a superstructure of laws, regulations, ethics and programs that include affirmative action and diversity training. Still, images manage to contaminate behavior, often subtly and ambiguously.

It happens in the Air Force, explained Edward Rice, a black B-52 pilot who was a lieutenant colonel and a White House Fellow when I met him several years ago. I asked him why, despite the military's exemplary record of opening doors to minorities, only about 300 of nearly 15,000 pilots in the Air Force were black. This shapes careers, since key commands are barred to Air Force officers who are not pilots. Why do many blacks wash out of flight school?

Rice offered a theory. In the cockpit with a black trainee, a white flight instructor must make split-second decisions about when to take control of the aircraft. If he thinks the trainee is flying dangerously, he will grab the stick. If in the back of the instructor's mind there lurks that age-old, widely held suspicion that blacks are less intelligent and less capable, perhaps he will move just a little more quickly to take control from a black trainee than from a white. And if he does that repeatedly, Rice noted, the black will not advance to the next level of training.

Consider another example. A white couple in northern California adopted a biracial girl as an infant. Their two biological children, both boys, were close in age, so all three youngsters attended the same high school at around the same time. When the white boys fell behind in class, notes and calls came home from teachers. But when the biracial girl had academic problems, there were no notes or calls. She looked black and hung out with black friends, and her parents concluded that the teachers had written her off.

Those teachers did not wear white hoods and stand in the schoolhouse door. They came from the mainstream of white America, where the images of blacks as less capable run strongly just beneath the surface of polite behavior. Even in the finest integrated schools across the country, I found black youngsters, pushed hard by their parents, who complained that white teachers made insufficient demands on them, assumed that they would be satisfied with less than A's, and discouraged them from taking honors courses or applying to top colleges.

Echoes of the Past

Decoding such encrypted racism is an uncertain art that requires a sense of history—the history of racial stereotyping in America—and a capacity to listen and observe how frequently the present echoes the past.

Many institutions that look integrated, for example, are often segregated within, for integration has largely meant the mere physical mixing of people of various races, not the sharing of power and the blending into an integral whole. Therefore, blacks who enter mostly white institutions often feel like invited guests—and not always very welcome guests—who are there at the pleasure of the whites. Rarely do the blacks attain ownership, authority, or the standing to set agendas. They are confronted by glass walls that whites often do not see.

A black man worked for IBM for three years before learning that every evening a happy hour was taking place in a nearby bar. Only white men from the office were involved—no women, no minorities. Had it been strictly social it would have been merely offensive. But it was also professionally damaging, for business was being done over drinks, plans were being designed, connections made. Excluded from that network, the black man was excluded from opportunity for advancement, and he left the job.

This is a common experience among blacks and women who have integrated the workplace, and it raises questions about possible remedies. Two come to mind: affirmative action and diversity training.

Sidewalk Bubblegum ©1996 Clay Butler. Used with permission.

Assume that the white men at the happy hour are not extreme racists, do not decide deliberately to exclude blacks and don't think about the implications of their gatherings at the bar. They go to the bar with people with whom they are most comfortable, and the most comfortable are people like themselves.

If an affirmative action plan were in place, promotions into management would be monitored by race and gender, and the marginalization of minorities and women—whether intentional or not—would become a matter of concern.

Just calling attention to the problem could be enough to make the white men conscious of the need to consider the black man for promotion. They might even reflect on how to bring him into the loop. Beyond that, diversity workshops, where office dynamics are discussed and minority employees can be heard, would highlight the happy hour as a tool of exclusion.

A Problem of Perception

The difficulty is that one has to perceive the problem to embrace the solutions. If you think that racism isn't harmful unless it wears sheets or burns crosses or bars blacks from motels and restaurants, you will support only the crudest anti-discrimination laws and not the more refined methods of affirmative action and diversity training. If you recognize how subtle racism can be, the subtler tools seem appropriate.

One of the great divides in the country is between those Americans who see only blatant racism and those who see the subtle forms as well. It is such a fundamental disagreement that it has shaped much of the current debate over affirmative action.

Opponents of affirmative action believe that prejudice and discrimination have diminished enough to have leveled the playing field for non-whites. The argument holds that affirmative action introduces unfairness and demeans non-whites by suggesting that they could not succeed without it.

Feeling Branded

Every solution, however, creates at least one new problem, and affirmative action is no exception. It is designed in principle to require that the best candidates be recruited from groups that have suffered discrimination. Nothing in the concept calls for the acceptance of unqualified people. Yet some managers have been so skittish about lawsuits or so eager to prove themselves non-racist that they have pushed certain black employees into jobs where they have foundered. That has played to the age-old stereotype of blacks as less competent than whites.

Many blacks complain about being branded with an assumption that without affirmative action they would not be in this college or on that construction crew or in that corporate office. Occasionally that reinforces self-doubt. A few black students at Princeton told me that when papers came due and exam time approached, they wondered if they really belonged at such a demanding school.

But it is wise to remember that these doubts—and even blacks' self-doubts—have existed for generations, since long before desegregation and affirmative action. The assumption that blacks were less able was a major reason that affirmative action was needed to overcome the obstacles to admitting, hiring and promoting them.

The old stereotype of blacks as unintelligent and lazy remains a constant as the remedy changes, and the constant hangs itself on whatever hook happens to be available. Before, it was said that blacks were unqualified and therefore weren't hired. Now, the argument goes, blacks are unqualified but are hired because they're black—same belief, different outcome.

If we have to choose—and apparently we do—it is the outcome that matters more than the belief. Would the black student rather be at Princeton and be thought less competent, or be thought less competent and *not* be at Princeton? Before affirmative action, Princeton and other top colleges admitted precious few blacks.

Another key criticism of affirmative action holds that it works against more qualified whites. Here again, the assumption is that whites are more qualified than blacks. Polls and focus groups have found that while most whites think that under affirmative action less qualified blacks are hired and promoted over more qualified whites, most blacks think that *without* affirmative action, less qualified *whites* are hired and promoted over more qualified *blacks*. Both sides want fairness, but each has a different notion of how to achieve it.

Surveys show that few whites can cite personal experience to justify their fears. With the total black population at just 13 percent, and a smaller percentage of blacks in a position to compete for jobs covered by affirmative action, the chance of edging out a more qualified white is slim. Moreover, even when a white person thinks he has been passed over for a less qualified black, he may be wrong. Some supervisors admit that they have told whites whom they didn't want to hire or promote, "I'd love to take you, but I've got to take a black—you know how it is." It's easier than telling the applicant that he doesn't measure up.

The Bottom Line

Paradoxically, just as affirmative action is being chipped away by the courts, legislators, and by voters in referendums, it is putting down deeper roots in colleges, corporations and government agencies. In many places, institutional ethics have evolved to the point where an all-white workforce or management team is automatically seen as inadequate and a diverse staff is seen as beneficial. The rationale has shifted from altruism to pragmatism, from high-minded compassion to bottom-line competition.

Business, for example, looks at the demographics of its potential employees and of its customers and reasons that it must diversify racially to profit. Colleges look at the world for which they're preparing students and conclude that a homogeneously white setting does not provide the best education. It may be sad, but morality is less potent than self-interest.

For the last 20 years, the military has managed race relations by emphasizing behavior, not beliefs. "You can think anything you want—that's your business," the military says to its members. "But what you do is our business. If you act in ways that deny opportunity on the basis of race, you interfere with the cohesiveness of the unit, and it becomes the concern of the service."

As practical as this is, it is a bit of a false dichotomy. Thoughts and actions interact with each other, cause each other, reinforce each other. And to assess behavior across racial lines, you have to keep coming back to beliefs as a reference point. It is not an institution's role to enforce certain beliefs on its students or employees, but in addressing racial dynamics the entrenched stereotypes need to be kept in mind. They illuminate and explain the actions.

Getting at the stereotypes requires some acknowledgment that whites benefit from racial prejudice, even as society suffers as a whole. Few white Americans reflect on the unseen privileges they possess or the greater sense of worth they acquire from their white skin. In addition to creating the traditional alignments of power in America, negative beliefs about blacks tend to enhance whites' self-esteem.

If blacks are less intelligent, in whites' belief, then it follows that whites are more intelligent. If blacks are lazier, whites are harder working. If blacks would prefer to live on welfare, then whites would prefer to be self-supporting. If blacks are more violent, whites are less violent—and the source of violence can be kept at a safe distance.

Many conservatives these days urge us to make an "optimistic" assessment of the racial situation. At the same time, they refuse to see the pernicious racism that persists. That blindness does not justify optimism. Legitimate optimism comes from facing the problems squarely and working to overcome the insidious subtleties of bigotry that still abide in the land.

"[There is no] single study to confirm the hypothesis that white racism harms blacks."

The Harm of White Racism Is Exaggerated

Robert Weissberg

There is no proof that blacks continue to be harmed by the racial prejudices of whites, contends Robert Weissberg in the following viewpoint. While many social analysts claim that white racism remains pervasive and continues to limit black progress, no solid evidence supports this theory. In fact, the author points out, many indicators—such as governmental efforts to redress past discrimination and the numerous black representatives selected by white-majority districts—suggest that white racism has largely subsided. Weissberg is a political science professor at the University of Illinois in Champaign-Urbana.

As you read, consider the following questions:

1. In Weissberg's opinion, the "science of white racism" is based on what three propositions?
2. According to the author, what is the main flaw in Joe R. Feagin's research claiming that white racism causes black attrition at predominantly white colleges?
3. In Weissberg's view, why has the theory of white racism gained so much acceptance?

Reprinted from "White Racism: The Seductive Lure of an Unproven Theory," by Robert Weissberg, *The Weekly Standard*, March 24, 1997, by permission of *The Weekly Standard*. Copyright, News America Incorporated.

In 1964, America's most eminent sociologist, Talcott Parsons, and its most eminent black academic, Kenneth Clark, collaborated on a magisterial tome called *The Negro American*. What is most striking about the book today, which is as dated as its title, is that it has no index entries for either "racism" or "white racism." Nor does Howard Ehrlich's 1973 work *The Social Psychology of Prejudice*, which reviewed 600-plus studies on ethnic prejudice. Differences between blacks and whites were thought to be caused by other forces, like the cultural legacy of slavery, unequal access to economic resources, educational inequities. The real culprit, as Ehrlich's title indicates, was not "white racism" but "prejudice," which was certainly considered a formidable impediment to black progress, but not a decisive one. Moreover, it was clear to all and sundry that prejudice was a condition of ignorance, for which education and ever greater interracial contact were the cure.

"White Racism" Is Popular

Today, of course, "white racism" is endlessly invoked, measured, dissected, and employed as an all-purpose explanation of African-American malaise. There are, perhaps, as many varieties of "white racism" as Eskimos have names for snow—"crypto-racism," "neo-racism," "meta-racism," and "kinetic racism," among many others. College administrators vie with black activists in passionately calling for anti-racism wars, while white liberals flagellate themselves and their fellow Caucasians.

Almost any failing can be, and has been, excused by "white racism." One study, for example, argued that a racist, sexist, Eurocentric bias in *mathematics* blocked the scientific and intellectual development of minorities. Traditional explanations of the absence of an entrepreneurial culture among American blacks, for example, are not only quickly dismissed, but the mere mention of them is itself considered evidence of a white-racist "mind-set."

After decades of false leads, it seems, the problem's root cause has been finally exposed. Compared with, say, the century or so it took for the public to accept the notion that germs cause disease, the embrace by universities, businesses, and government of the "white racism" explanation took but a historical millisecond. Why the dramatic change? There are two possible explanations for the sudden popularity of the "white racism" argument. One is scientific: Empirical evidence proves it. The other is that the "white racism" argument is politically convenient. Let me address each in turn.

The Science of White Racism

The science of white racism is based on three simple propositions. The first is that nearly all whites, consciously or unconsciously, hold negative views of blacks. These views vary from old-fashioned stereotypes—e.g., blacks are childlike and excitable—to pseudoscientific notions—e.g., blacks are genetically less intelligent.

The second proposition is that these ideas deeply permeate society, are transmitted by books, films, art, music, and wherever else information is conveyed, and are implicitly written into our laws and institutional arrangements. All together, this constitutes white racism on a grand cultural scale.

The final and critical proposition is that white-racist beliefs are readily absorbed by blacks themselves and work their destructive power from the inside out. At its core, the incapacitation is psychological. White racism is a cognitive virus, inculated by whites and passed on to blacks, that eventually creates the all-too-familiar tangle of pathologies.

Clearly, many whites harbor negative images of blacks. And it is equally true that many blacks passionately believe their difficulties flow from white racism. But to my knowledge, no scientific research demonstrates how white racism—as a mental state among *whites*—incapacitates blacks. *PsycINFO*, a database that covers the field of psychology, features 87 entries from 1967 to 1995 when you use the keywords "white racism." None of these studies, however, attempts to explain just how white racism operates; its negative impact is merely assumed. Books by Cornel West, Derrick Bell, and others who analyze the destructive costs of white racism are likewise mute when it comes to offering hard evidence. Nor have inquiries to fellow scholars concerned with this subject elicited help in finding a single study to confirm the hypothesis that white racism harms blacks.

Joe Feagin's Research

To appreciate the unsound empirical foundation of white racism's impact, consider one purported example of its documentation. It is offered by a well-published, Harvard-trained research professor at the University of Florida, appears in a scholarly journal, and is allegedly scientific in design. In "The Continuing Significance of Racism," published in the June 1992 *Journal of Black Studies*, Joe R. Feagin asks the question: What explains growing black attrition at predominantly white colleges? After reviewing other possible explanations—lack of financial aid, family deterioration, growing drug use, a disdain for education—Feagin sets off to demonstrate that the real culprit is the racist environment at white-dominated colleges and the ways in which blacks on campus routinely encounter debilitating hostility from white students, professors, administrators, even alumni.

Almost 200 middle-class African Americans were interviewed during 1988–89 to determine the source of the black exodus from college. Unpleasant memories are the only data Feagin presents. The views of relevant whites and other potentially pertinent information—academic records, for example—are not supplied. The interpretations of the black ex-students are not challenged, and corroborating details are not solicited.

A few such encounters are objectively hostile acts—being called "nigger" in public, for example, or racially charged encounters with police. Such clearly defined hostility might well have a negative impact on academic performance. But such hostility is the exception, not the rule, in Feagin's research. Most professors would recognize the vast majority of Feagin's tales if they came from white students: They are the lame, desperate excuses common to the academically and personally troubled. Several respondents complain about feeling unarticulated aversion to their personal features, like black hair or black speech inflection. Others believe they are not being treated as distinctive individuals. White professors made students feel bad by fretting about their poor attendance and correcting their English.

But in Feagin's research all these woes—remarkably similar to the woes of the adolescent in every novel, every television show, every cliché, trying to find a place for himself or herself in a cold, cruel world—are considered the result of white racism. It was, Feagin says, a ceaseless part of campus life, permeating everything from the secret meaning of casual conversations to the official "white" literary style. The campus environment cannot help but take an enervating toll. After experiencing all the unexpressed, nearly imperceptible, but "real" antagonism towards their very blackness, black students find dropping out a survival technique.

In legal language, these are all unsupported accusations—no evidence is offered of malice, physical intimidation, or slander. But this is the very nature of the charge of white racism. When we are asked to consider whether someone was discriminated against, we can do so because discrimination is objective in character. An academically well-qualified black who is denied admission to a college that accepts less qualified whites could justifiably claim discrimination based on race.

A Subjectively Defined Racism

But white racism is subjective by definition. According to Feagin and its other theorists, even though white racism may be invisible to all but the recipient, if the recipient *feels* it, the feeling itself validates the existence of the phenomenon. The *intent* of the white racist is irrelevant; for example, a white teacher disproportionately praising black students might be guilty of racism if blacks sense that the praise is given solely because they are black. Because of white racism's fundamentally subjective character, anti-discrimination laws aimed at overt behavior cannot banish it even if such laws are effective. Therefore, eliminating bias in and of itself cannot bring racial harmony.

Not only does the white-racism theory lack scientific support, its deficiencies are obvious. Contradictory evidence abounds. Thomas Sowell has pointed out that blacks from the British West Indies exceed both native black Americans *and whites* in their professional and economic attainment. If white racism is so deeply ingrained, how can we explain all the white-dominated government and corporate efforts to ameliorate past discrimination? What about all the blacks elected in cities and congressional districts with white majorities? Nor can all the poll data depicting the absence of racist views among whites be ignored.

What is especially remarkable is the contrast between the intensive scrutiny given *The Bell Curve* and other statistical examinations of racial differences and the credulousness with which the white-racism theory has been treated. While *The Bell Curve* and its variants have produced an industry of hostile symposia placing every shred of evidence under a microscope, the white-racism theory escapes inspection.

This is hardly accidental.

Why the Theory of White Racism Is Accepted

If white racism is such a frail explanation, why does it have such cultural reach? Why do social scientists, who are so expert at devastating flimsy arguments, buy it so unquestionably? Why are white public officials, even outspoken conservatives, silent when society's racism is invoked as an all-purpose explanation of our ills? The answer is simple: The white-racism theory of injury has enormous appeal—*to whites themselves.* The theory's allure rests on its political and psychological utility.

First, consider simple monetary costs: "Curing" white racism may not work, but white-racism theorists themselves can be bought off pretty cheaply. Balance the outlays for diversity workshops, cosmetic educational adjustments, modifying public vocabulary, and other largely symbolic anti-racist gestures with, say, creating effective social-welfare programs, guaranteeing educational attainment, or strictly enforcing the criminal code, and you see how it works.

Imagine a college dean who is under pressure to ensure the graduation of hundreds of poorly prepared minority students. That is a formidable task; progress would be expensive, the labor would be intensive, and the result uncertain. But if this savvy bureaucrat proclaims white racism the culprit, one that can be conveniently addressed by mandatory four-hour sensitivity workshops, his burden lightens immeasurably.

There is no end to the novelties our college dean could

propose to satisfy the white-racism theorists. An /
American cultural center. A few multicultural c
maybe even a sub-discipline. And, of course, if he
these solutions, that resistance will help confirm
racism's lingering, tenacious grip on *him*.

Letting Go of Race

The dissolution of the color line is already happening, i
terracial marriages and adoptions, in polling booths, ii
unexpected resonance of Tiger Woods's 'Cablinasian'
dle, in popular culture. The ground is shifting undei
feet. We should embrace the fact that it's happening
shouldn't fear that if race lost all its value as a distin
among people we would suddenly have nothing to s
Human beings are deeper and more protean than that.
the development of an American civilization or culture
thy of that depth depends on our letting go of race as it
ganizing principle.

Jim Sleeper, quoted in *American Enterprise*, November/December 199

Those who choose to face race issues head-on must
the eventuality of well-publicized marches, demonsti
takeovers, lists of non-negotiable demands, lawsuit;
cotts, and possible acts of violence. Thus, agreeing wi
itants that white racism is to blame should be conside
act of *diplomacy*.

The theory offers well-meaning whites easy sa
compared with previous redemptive paths. Since, acc
to the theory, black problems originate in white min
responsibility of whites is to think "good thoughts." /
ment and a state of grace are achieved by using the
terminology (e.g., "African-American community
"black neighborhood") and disassociating from an
critical of the white-racism theory. Thus, on a college
pus, reading *The Bell Curve* is itself a sin. By expungin
gerous negative stereotypes and inappropriate cultural
tations, whites can achieve a form of earthly salvation-
as other responsibilities seem to lighten. The obligati
the 1960s—sending kids to integrated schools, maki
nancial donations, occasionally walking a picket lin
now unnecessary. Indeed, these once-virtuous gesture

actually reflect the white-racist idea that blacks cannot manage their own struggle!

The white-racism theory excuses whites of the 1990s from the good deeds that offered salvation in the 1960s. They no longer have to participate in interracial dating. They need not seek out black friends or fund civil-rights organizations. Instead, they can perfect their attitudes privately.

Incurable Guilt

And for those old-fashioned white liberals from the 1960s, the white-racism theory is deliverance. It drives out more disturbing, awkward, and embarrassing explanations of racial differences in outcomes that were not supposed to persist after the efforts of the Great Society were undertaken. How do they reconcile $5 trillion in Great Society programs with the decimated black family and a ghetto in worse condition than it was before the 1960s?

The white-racism theory offers the answer. Not only does it bestow responsibility "where it belongs," but the guilt is virtually immutable, incurable. The masochistic liberal may have an impeccable public record, but he knows his racist soul to be beyond purification. After all, doesn't he avoid rundown black neighborhoods? Doesn't he fear lower-class black males when they pass him on the street? Such uncontrolled reactions confirm the key element in the white-racism argument: All whites, regardless of deeds and denials, harbor anti-black feeling. Authoritatively telling a 1960s liberal that he suffers from racism is like telling a hypochondriac that he is ill.

The white-racism theory has created a booming business for whites and blacks alike—those skilled at hunting white racism down, exposing its destructive power, and hectoring its perpetrators. It offers them a lucrative lifetime career in academia and diversity-counseling and provides similar remuneration to the bureaucrats who hire them. Governments have no choice but to create paid task forces to examine school textbooks, curriculums, even school disciplinary actions. Though these expenditures constitute little more than high-minded extortion, they can be publicly justified as a small price to pay for the promise of racial peace.

Thus, the white-racism argument offers something for everybody. Even conservative unbelievers may (privately) acknowledge that its official acceptance maintains an uneasy social peace without leading to skyrocketing deficits. Realistic liberals frustrated by government's failure receive some psychological comfort: Social-welfare expansion, court-imposed integration edicts, anti-discrimination laws, preferential-treatment programs, and so on were good, well-intentioned ideas, but they could do nothing about the true sickness.

Something for everybody—yes, except the black kids in Feagin's study and their cohorts who are sentenced to a lifetime of believing that they are hated, that they will always be hated, and that there is nothing they can do about it.

> "*Race is a major factor in police decisions to follow, detain, search, arrest—and of course, to beat up or torture—suspects.*"

Racial Bias Influences Law Enforcement Decisions

Keeanga-Yamahtta Taylor

Racism influences law enforcement and criminal justice decisions, argues Keeanga-Yamahtta Taylor in the following viewpoint. Minorities who have committed no crimes, especially African American males, are disproportionately stopped, searched, and detained by police. Blacks are much more likely than whites to be brutalized or killed by police officers; moreover, they are incarcerated at six times the rate of whites. Taylor is a freelance writer.

As you read, consider the following questions:
1. In Taylor's opinion, why did the case of Amadou Diallo draw national attention?
2. Blacks account for what percentage of all traffic stops, according to the author?
3. What percentage of the prison and jail population is composed of blacks, according to Taylor?

Excerpted from "Racism and the Criminal Injustice System," by Keeanga-Yamahtta Taylor, *International Socialist Review*, Summer 1999. Reprinted with permission.

On the night of February 4, 1999, Amadou Diallo had his first—and tragically his last—brush with the American criminal justice system. Diallo's family will not quickly or easily forget the encounter, nor will the many hundreds of thousands of people across the country who were outraged and moved to protest the latest victim of New York's finest. Four white NYPD officers shot at Diallo, an African immigrant, 41 times. The officers were searching for an anonymous "Black rapist." When they came across Diallo, he fit the profile—he was young, Black, male. Of the 41 bullets fired, 19 ripped through Diallo and killed him on the spot.

Diallo's case drew national attention not only because of the uncontrolled brutality of the police officers involved, but also because Diallo obviously wasn't guilty of any wrongdoing. But his case is certainly not exceptional.

Police Abuse Is the Rule

Investigation into the Diallo case has confirmed what activists and people from the neighborhoods have been saying for a long time—abuse and brutality are not the exception or random acts of violence, but rather they are the rule. The cops who fired 41 bullets at Diallo were from the Special Crimes Unit, which in one year stopped more than 45,000 people—most of them Black or Latino—but arrested fewer than 10,000.

In Illinois, a group of death row inmates, known as the Death Row Ten, languish in prison, although most of them were convicted solely on the basis of "confessions" that were beaten or tortured out of them by racist and corrupt cops.

Blacks make up 14 percent of drivers, yet account for 72 percent of all traffic stops. Ron Hampton, a retired police officer and executive director of the National Black Police Association, told Amnesty International in 1998, "In a training video, every criminal portrayed is black."

Both Amnesty International and Human Rights Watch have condemned American police departments as dens of racism, brutality and corruption. Officers violate the law they are supposed to uphold with impunity. According to Amnesty:

> . . . in the past eight years independent inquiries have uncovered systematic abuses in some of the country's largest city

police departments, revealing a serious nationwide problem. In each case the authorities had ignored long-standing and routine police brutality in high crime districts. Many of these cities have had histories of police brutality and corruption, with periodic scandals followed by reform initiatives; the emphasis on the "war on crime" in recent years has reportedly contributed to more aggressive policing in many areas.

The warehousing of Blacks in U.S. prisons stands as a terrible indictment of U.S. racism. It is also becoming a civil rights crisis. For most of U.S. history, Blacks have fought for and won elementary human rights, including the right to vote. Yet today, more than 1.4 million Black men—13 percent of the African-American male population—have lost their right to vote because of felony convictions.

A Deeply Racist Society

The U.S. is one of the most racist, unequal and unjust societies in the world. Of all industrialized countries, it has the greatest disparity between rich and poor. The rich are usually superrich, while the poor suffer from unthinkable deprivation. In 1973, 11 percent of families with children under 18 were poor. By 1995, in the midst of the much-lauded economic boom, that number swelled to more than 16 percent. In 1995, nearly half of poor Black children were living below 50 percent of the federal poverty level. There were half a million more poor married couples in 1995 than in 1973. Over the same period, 3 million more people worked at least part time, and a million more worked full time, year-round.

Crime thrives in these conditions. As the Justice Department put it in 1967: "Crime flourishes where the conditions of life are worst." The "foundation of a national strategy against crime," therefore, had to be "an unremitting national effort for social justice." But blaming poverty alone for the rates of incarceration of Blacks misses the way in which racism pervades the entire system and discriminates against Blacks in particular. The U.S. imprisons Black men at a rate six times that of white men. Black males make up less than 7 percent of the U.S. population, yet they comprise almost half of the prison and jail population.

Relative to population size, about five times as many African Americans as whites are arrested for the serious

Horsey. Reprinted with special permission from King Features Syndicate.

crimes of murder, rape, robbery and aggravated assault. About three times as many African Americans as whites are arrested for less serious crimes, which account for the bulk of arrests flooding the criminal justice system. If no racial bias exists in the criminal justice system, then the racial makeup of the prison population should at least roughly reflect the racial disparity in arrest rates. If three times as many African Americans are arrested for less serious crimes, then there should be roughly three times as many African Americans per capita incarcerated for those crimes. But the racial disparity between African Americans and whites in prison is overwhelmingly wider than arrest rates suggest it should be. There are seven African Americans to each white in prison. . . .

Race Is a Factor in Police Decisions

The first experience with the criminal justice system for many Blacks in this country is a run-in with the police. Racism is most obvious in the attitudes that police departments have towards Blacks in general. Almost any serious study reveals that race is a major factor in police decisions to follow, detain, search, arrest—and of course, to beat up or torture—suspects. A California study showed that the rate of unfounded arrests—in which the suspect is clearly innocent, or evidence is insufficient or illegally obtained—among Blacks was four times that of whites. In Oakland, the rate was 12 times the rate for whites. In Los Angeles, the rate was seven times as great, and in San Diego the rate was six times that of whites.

The State of Maryland recently paid $50,000 to a Black Harvard Law School graduate and his family after state police stopped their rented Cadillac and conducted an illegal search. Police stopped the man because he fit a police "profile" of the "typical" drug dealer: a Black male driving a luxury vehicle on an interstate highway. Police in Denver compiled a list of suspected gang members: it contained the names of two out of three African-American youths in the entire city between the ages of 12 and 24. Even though the police suspected only 250 gang members in the city, the list grew to include 5,500 names. More than 93 percent of the people on the list were African-American or Hispanic teenagers.

Blacks are 10 times more likely than whites to be shot by police, according to Harvard law professor Charles Ogletree. And as the war on crime recruits more foot soldiers, those odds are likely to worsen. Between 1980 and 1990, the number of police officers doubled in the U.S. In addition to the 554,000 officers employed by local and state police forces, there are now 1.5 million private security officers. This can only result in a higher number of confrontations between police and Black civilians, producing more outrages like the murder of Amadou Diallo.

"Like so many other destructive racial myths, the myth of the racist cop refuses to die."

Racial Bias Does Not Influence Most Law Enforcement Decisions

Part I: Jared Taylor; Part II: Walter Williams

The authors of the following two-part viewpoint maintain that claims of racial bias in law enforcement are grossly exaggerated. In Part I, journalist and commentator Jared Taylor contends that police arrest blacks and Latinos more than whites simply because these minorities commit a disproportionate amount of crimes. In Part II, syndicated columnist Walter Williams argues that race is often a reliable indicator for police as they target potential criminals.

As you read, consider the following questions:
1. What reliable evidence reveals that blacks and Hispanics use drugs at higher rates than whites do, according to Taylor?
2. According to Williams, why did the governor of New Jersey fire the state's police superintendent?
3. According to the 1997 FBI Uniform Crime Report, cited by Williams, what percentage of drug arrests that year involved minorities?

Part I: Reprinted from "Police Bias? Says Who?" by Jared Taylor, *American Renaissance*, July 1999, with permission from *American Renaissance*, www.amren.com. Part II: Reprinted from Walter Williams, "Racial Profiling Puzzle," *The Washington Times*, March 14, 1999, by permission of Walter Williams and Creators Syndicate, Inc.

I

The "racist" police officer is practically a cliché. White cops all over the country are supposed to be shooting, beating, and arresting innocent blacks and Hispanics—or at least trying a whole lot harder to collar them than whites. Aside from some isolated incidents of racially motivated brutality, this is a false image. The police arrest blacks and Hispanics because they commit crimes.

No Evidence of Pervasive Bias

The first line of evidence is the close correspondence between survey data and arrest data. If the public says half the muggers are black, and half the muggers the police arrest are black, it is unlikely the police are making "biased" arrests. Even more to the point, the police have essentially no discretion over whom they arrest for a violent crime. Except for murder victims, most people get a good enough look at an assailant to know if he is black or white. If the victim says a white man took his wallet, the police can't very well go out and arrest a black man even if they wanted to.

The police have a lot of discretion over whether to make an arrest in the case of non-violent crimes, such as violation of liquor laws. Unlike murder or rape, there is not a great deal of public pressure to make arrests, and the police can walk away from crime if they want to. Presumably, a "racist" officer would see a drunk on the street and make an arrest only if the drunk were black. In fact, drunk driving and other liquor offenses—in which police can make arrests or not largely as they choose—are the very crimes for which the black multiple of the white arrest rate is the smallest. If "racist" cops are picking on blacks they are not doing a good job.

Finally, if the police are "racist," why are Asians arrested at consistently lower rates than whites? Wouldn't "racist" cops think of some way to snare Asians?

It is often argued that the large number of blacks arrested for drugs—particularly crack cocaine—is evidence of police bias. However, there is a completely independent indicator of who is using illegal drugs, which suggests that the police are arresting the very people they should. The Department of Health and Human Services keeps statistics on people admitted to emergency rooms because of drug overdoses. Blacks are admitted at 6.67 times the white rate for heroin and morphine, and no less than 10.5 times the white rate for cocaine (Hispanics are admitted at two to three times the white rate). What better evidence could there be that people of different races are using drugs at markedly different rates, and that the police are simply doing their job?

Like so many other destructive racial myths, the myth of the racist cop refuses to die.

II

New Jersey Gov. Christine Todd Whitman fired Col. Carl Williams, her state police superintendent, after he told reporters minority groups were more likely to be involved in drug trafficking. Col. Williams was already under fire by black ministers and civil-rights groups accusing the State Police of racial profiling, a practice of targeting minority drivers for traffic stops and searches in the war against drug trafficking.

Mrs. Whitman said she fired Col. Williams because his comments "are inconsistent with our efforts to enhance public confidence in the State Police." Let's look at racial profiling.

If God were a state trooper, He wouldn't be involved with the imperfection and indignity of racial profiling—not because He's good but because He knows all. God would know who is a drug trafficker and who's not.

Race Is a Useful Indicator

Mere mortals like us don't know everything. Unlike God, we face a world of costly and incomplete information, and that means we have to do a lot of guessing and playing hunches. Part of that strategy requires the use of indicators that have varying degrees of reliability. Physical characteristics, including race, are among those indicators that can tell us things. Thus, we can benefit from learning to employ cheap-to-observe characteristics as proxies for more-costly-to-observe characteristics. Race is a cheap-to-observe characteristic that, while imperfect, is nonetheless sometimes useful.

I've hailed taxis in downtown D.C. at night, only to watch the driver pass me up and pick up a white passenger down the street. As often as not, the driver was black. Was the driver a racist? Or was he using my skin color as a proxy for an undesirable destination such as a high-crime neighborhood or as a proxy for the probability of being robbed? He was racially profiling me, but he was wrong in my case. It is never pleasant to be a victim of racial profiling, but whom should I blame: the taxi driver who's not God and is simply doing what he can to protect himself? Or should I blame black thugs who prey on taxi drivers, making them leery about picking up black customers at night?

Probable Cause

There is one essential safeguard against racial profiling during traffic stops already in place. It is called probable cause. If an individual, whether that person be African-American, Caucasian, Latino—or a member of any other racial or ethnic group—has been pulled over by an officer with probable cause to make that traffic stop and it turns out that individual has done nothing wrong, then that person is free to go. As a society, sometimes law-abiding citizens will be inconvenienced when police aggressively enforce laws and investigate crimes. Just being stopped by the police when they have good reason to do so should not cause those stopped to believe that their rights were violated.

Robert T. Scully, *Washington Times*, June 14, 1999.

My physician practices racial profiling. Even though my PSA [prostate-specific androgen] is 2.3, he is very aggressive about the slightest change. He's also aggressive about treating my mildly elevated blood pressure. He doesn't know anything certain about my individual risk of prostate cancer and hypertension-related diseases. Not being God, he uses the medical evidence about blacks in general to make guesses about me. Should I take a cue from Mrs. Whitman and fire him for making assumptions about me based upon my race?

There Is a High Probability That Criminals Are Black

What about racial assumptions the New Jersey State Police may make? According to the 1997 FBI Uniform Crime Report, 63 percent of the 65,624 drug arrests were minorities (50 percent blacks and 13 percent Hispanics). Since blacks are only 13 percent of the total population, it means law enforcement officials can assign a higher probability that a drug trafficker is a black more so than other racial groups. In terms of arresting drug traffickers, doing disproportionate traffic stops on blacks will have a higher payoff than traffic stops on say Japanese, Russian Orthodox Jews or 75-year-olds.

Statistics about the grossly disproportionate number of blacks involved in drug trafficking is no comfort to the law-abiding black who is stopped and searched. It's humiliating and demeaning, not to mention inconvenient. But with whom should we be angry: police officers or those who've made black synonymous with crime? Of course, an alternative is not to stop cars at all.

> *"Industries realized that there are fewer and fewer places they could pollute freely and targeted minority communities as a place to do so."*

Environmental Racism Endangers Minorities

Edward Rush

In the following viewpoint, Edward Rush argues that sources of toxic pollution are disproportionately located in minority communities. Blacks, Latinos, and Native Americans are therefore more likely to live near dumps and waste sites than are whites—and as a result experience higher rates of illnesses and birth defects. This kind of discrimination, termed "environmental racism," has been challenged by the environmental justice movement. However, Rush points out, several industries are trying to discredit this movement by publishing faulty studies claiming that environmental racism does not exist. Rush is an organizer with the Center for Health, Environment, and Justice in Falls Church, Virginia.

As you read, consider the following questions:
1. According to Rush, how does environmental inequity develop into environmental racism?
2. What are some of the flaws of the University of Chicago study on environmental injustice, according to the author?
3. In Rush's opinion, what two steps should the environmental justice movement take to counter its opponents?

Reprinted, with permission, from "Environmental Racism: Fact and Friction," by Edward Rush, *Everyone's Backyard*, Summer 1997.

A recent University of Chicago study concluded that in Chicago, blacks were *less likely* to live close to dumps, factories and waste sites than whites. The study also states that young white professionals are relocating near industrial sites to take advantage of loft apartments in abandoned factories. The *Chicago Tribune* even went so far as to write an editorial based on the study entitled, "Doubts About a Racism Theory." In the editorial, the researchers from the university are praised for their service to mankind, and it is concluded that more studies should be done on environmental racism throughout the country. The inference is that more studies are needed that conclude that this whole environmental racism scare is not real. It is just a case of misinterpreting data. This study is the opening salvo in an effort to win back the ideological high ground for polluting industries, and make excuses for regulatory agencies. It should come as no surprise that the concept of environmental racism has come under attack. It was only a matter of time.

Seemingly, no one would attack the notion of environmental justice. After all, freedom, liberty and justice for all are the tenets upon which this country is supposedly built, right? However, as far as Environmental Protection Agency (EPA) officials and polluting industry executives were concerned, until President Bill Clinton signed the executive order in 1994 directing government agencies to make it part of their mission, environmental justice was just a concept—a concept put forth and championed by a racial fringe with very little political muscle. However, when grassroots groups like the Ironbound Committee on Toxic Waste in Newark, New Jersey, and the Citizens Against Toxic Exposure in Pensacola, Florida, started using the executive order as a tool in winning their environmental battles, polluters and their scientists developed a counterattack. Industries realized that there are fewer and fewer places they could pollute freely and targeted minority communities as a place to do so. They began to mount a public campaign to counter the charge that environmental racism is a factor in deciding which communities get dumped on.

Discrediting Environmental Justice

This campaign to discredit the existence of environmental racism is not about science, nor is it motivated by the desire to produce scholarly research. It is an attempt to shift the public discourse to a debate over whether the premise of environmental racism is even valid. The intention is to bog down the proponents of environmental justice with a need to defend their existence, and convince those who are on the fence about this issue that it is an imaginary problem. These tactics aren't new. Arguments of a similar nature have been made by opponents of affirmative action who believe that job or college placement slots set aside for women and racial minorities are unfair. In this argument and in the argument against environmental racism, opponents base their opposition on a false belief that prejudices do not exist.

Companies that create special burdens for the communities around their facilities point out that besides the fact that they produce products or services that people need, they do not site their facilities with a racial prejudice in mind. This claim is echoed by industry studies that supposedly prove that environmental injustices do not exist. These studies will state emphatically their conclusions are based on 'objective' information collected by 'objective' researchers. As such, they proclaim their conclusions to be infallible. Unfortunately, this is often not the case, as shown by the American Society of Mechanical Engineers study (Rigo 1995), which was funded partly with $150,000 from the Vinyl Institute. This study concluded that there is no correlation between chlorine entering a combustion process and dioxin exiting it. However, using Rigo's own data, Greenpeace scientist Pat Costner concluded that the study actually supported a correlation between chlorine input and dioxin output. This situation is similar to the University of Chicago study that finds that no "environmental injustice intent" exists in Chicago. Perhaps the executives of the company that built the Robbins incinerator intended to have the incinerator spew toxins into their own bedroom windows and instead, it ended up spewing toxins into the Robbins housing projects. The fact that the incinerator was built in an area of Robbins where a disproportionate number of poor minorities live is merely a coincidence, right? Wrong. The implication of the studies and industry propaganda is that the belief in environmental racism stems from bad science at best and racial paranoia at worst.

However it came to be, industry and EPA documents contradict assertions that people of color do not suffer disproportionately from the siting of polluting facilities. In addition, information and propaganda that is disseminated in support of waste and polluting facilities is much less compelling when environmental racism is put in the proper context.

The Result of a Power Dynamic

Environmental racism is not science, but the result of a power dynamic. The dynamic that causes environmental inequity occurs when people who have power in a society choose not to have environmental hazards in their community. This environmental inequity becomes environmental injustice when environmental hazards are placed in a community of disempowered people. Furthermore, environmental injustice develops into environmental racism when people in that community happen to fall into a different racial classification than those in power. Coincidentally, or perhaps not so coincidentally, the people in American society who tend to be disempowered most often are Native Americans, Latino peoples, people of Afrikan descent, and other racial minorities. Science is simply a tool by which to measure the results of discrimination, and a blunt tool at that. Part of the reason the tools are inadequate is because a study that charts how close people live to waste sites does not take into account where the people get their food, their ability to relocate, or whether they had any say in the siting of the facility in the first place. Lastly, but most importantly, a study designed in this way doesn't tell us who is getting sick and dying from environmental exposures. All of these are factors in the dynamics of power, yet none of these factors are addressed in the University of Chicago study.

The fact is that the University of Chicago study is based in part on historical data that is highly irrelevant. There was relatively no public consciousness of industrial facilities causing health hazards before the late 1970s. So, data indi-

Environmental Injustice

A widely cited study of U.S. Census data by the National Association for the Advancement of Colored People and the United Church of Christ Commission for Racial Justice found that people of color were 47 percent more likely than whites to live near a commercial hazardous-waste facility. The study also found that the percentage of minorities was three times higher in areas with high concentrations of such facilities than in areas without them. Moreover, the study suggested that minorities' exposure to environmental toxins was getting worse. . . .

Even air pollution affects minorities disproportionately, according to the Environmental Protection Agency. The 437 counties and independent cities that failed to meet air-quality standards in 1990, for example, are home to 80 percent of the nation's Hispanics and 65 percent of African-Americans but just 57 percent of all whites.

Mary H. Cooper, *CQ Researcher*, June 19, 1998.

cating that mostly whites lived near factories in the 1960s doesn't tell us much. If the noise and the stench from the facility got to be too much, then invariably the white folks would move away, and those who could not afford to move or those who previously were not shown property in the area would move in, because that is where they could afford to live. It defies logic and common sense to suggest that white professionals who can relocate almost anywhere would choose to move to a location that would be highly toxic. This would lead one to believe that the former industrial areas mentioned in the University of Chicago report no longer pose any serious health threats. If this is not the case, then the group that should have the most thanks for the researchers of this report are the realtors of the greater Chicago area. This kind of information should provide at least a short term boom as all the yuppies relocate to different parts of the city. After all, what better way to depopulate an area than to suggest that living there will cause residents to die of cancer and have children born with birth defects. When people don't move after learning that they live in an area that is contaminated, it is because they can't afford to, not because they prefer to stay.

Addressing a Persistent Problem

Environmental racism is fact, not fiction. Unfortunately, it will remain with us until the environment is dealt with in a different way in our society. As long as the attitude persists that one can foul or poison a small part of the planet where 'other' people live without any negative consequence to themselves, then the problem of environmental inequity will persist. As long as people of color are less empowered, then they will be that 'other.' The key to countering this bit of deceit designed to derail the environmental justice movement is twofold: first, the movement must continue to move forward in a determined effort to make the environment clean and safe for all people. Secondly, there must be a unified response to the inevitable attacks on the validity of the need for an environmental justice movement, with fervor, diligence and speed.

> "*The cry of 'environmental racism,' buoyed by misleading research, is belied by more careful studies.*"

Claims of Environmental Racism Are Unfounded

Christopher H. Foreman Jr.

Since the 1980s, the "environmental justice" (EJ) movement has claimed that industrial polluters and waste facilities are more likely to locate near minority or low-income populations. In the following viewpoint, Christopher H. Foreman Jr. argues that such charges are mostly groundless. Several studies making claims about environmental racism are flawed or have been disproven, the author maintains. Furthermore, the EJ movement is more concerned about grassroots egalitarianism than it is about serious public health issues. Foreman is a senior fellow at the Brookings Institution.

As you read, consider the following questions:
1. What incident first brought recognition to the environmental justice movement, according to the author?
2. According to Foreman, what did the U.S. Government Accounting Office conclude in its largely ignored 1995 study on municipal landfills?
3. In Foreman's opinion, what are the fundamental ideals of the environmental justice movement?

Reprinted from ". . . And 'Environmental Justice' for All?" by Christopher H. Foreman Jr., *Priorities*, vol. 9, no. 4 (1997), by permission of the American Council on Science and Health.

On February 11, 1994, President Bill Clinton issued an executive order titled "Federal Actions to Address Environmental Justice in Minority and Low Income Populations." The administration therewith announced that the Environmental Protection Agency (EPA) and other federal programs would begin "identifying and addressing, as appropriate, disproportionately high and adverse human health or environmental effects . . . on minority populations and low-income populations in the United States."

Described thus, "environmental justice" (also called "environmental equity") certainly *seems* a reasonable concern. After all, minorities and low-income persons suffer disproportionately from many illnesses and often cannot obtain adequate health care. And because lack of money or education can seriously limit residential and employment options, such persons might have more difficulty avoiding polluted localities. Moreover, communities populated largely by minorities or low-income persons might be politically weak and thus more susceptible than affluent neighborhoods to becoming locales for dumps, waste-treatment plants, and other land uses unwanted by residents in the vicinity. And if pollution causes disease, such susceptibility could be very important.

A Movement Is Born

But some troubling misconceptions accompany these plausible arguments. The executive order and related EPA policy innovations stemmed from allegations by the "environmental justice" (EJ) movement of institutionalized "environmental racism."

The EJ movement is a diverse coalition of "people of color" grassroots organizations and their allies. EJ activism, like most other forms of grassroots environmentalism, differs somewhat from traditional—"hiking, biking, and spotted owls"—environmentalism. Escalating public concern about toxic pollutants (especially hazardous waste) in the wake of the Love Canal scare of 1980, and the costly congressional overreaction to that scare (Superfund), heightened the visibility and credibility of appeals based on purported environmental hazards in minority communities.

Suddenly, environmentalism wasn't just a "middle-class

white folks" issue. The EJ movement made its first splash in 1982, with a protest against a proposed landfill for PCB [polychlorinated biphenyl]-contaminated soil in Warren County, North Carolina. Hundreds of demonstrators were arrested in the failed endeavor to prevent the landfill. District of Columbia Congressional delegate Walter Fauntroy returned from Warren County to spur the U.S. General Accounting Office (GAO), an investigative arm of Congress, to pursue an inquiry.

Shallow Evidence

The GAO found that predominately Black communities were the sites of three of the four "offsite" (i.e., not adjacent to or part of an industrial facility) hazardous-waste landfills in a region comprising eight southeastern states. That the GAO could not address whether these landfills would affect the health of the populations living near them did not deter the activists from using the GAO's findings as evidence of significant pollution-burden disparities between races and between income groups.

In 1987, a few years after the release of the GAO report, the United Church of Christ (UCC)'s Commission for Racial Justice unveiled *Toxic Wastes and Race in the United States: A National Report on the Racial and Socio-Economic Characteristics of Communities with Hazardous Waste Sites*—a classic of advocacy research (research influenced by outcome preference and a policy agenda)—at the National Press Club, in Washington, DC. The UCC report—which had not undergone prepublication peer review—suggested a correlation between race and the likelihood of living near either a commercial hazardous-waste facility or an "uncontrolled" toxic-waste site: "Residential ZIP code areas with the highest number of commercial hazardous waste facilities also had the highest mean percentage" of minority residents. According to the report, minorities averaged 24 percent of the total population in ZIP Code (postal-delivery) areas with a commercial hazardous-waste facility, but in ZIP Code areas without such a facility minorities averaged only 12 percent.

But the UCC report also stated, in passing, that more than half the population of the United States lived in ZIP

Code areas with a commercial hazardous-waste facility. In any case, such facilities process only a small fraction (perhaps 4 percent) of all hazardous waste in the United States. The UCC report did not provide a comprehensive picture of the distribution of hazardous waste in the U.S., much less evidence of social disparity in that distribution. Moreover, the report did not provide any information on exposure, much less on the possible health consequences thereof.

Little Evidence for Environmental Racism

"Environmental racism" is not responsible for the prevalence of industrial facilities in lower income communities.

Studies that examined historical land-use patterns and neighborhood composition at the time the facilities were sited found little, if any, evidence that siting and permitting decisions are responsible for the existence of industrial facilities in low-income and minority communities. Rather, they have found that the prevalence of industrial facilities in particular areas has tended to drive down neighboring property values, encouraging those who can afford it to move to more desirable neighborhoods, and inducing an influx of low-income residents.

Jonathan H. Adler, *CEI Update*, May 1998.

The UCC report also suggested that minorities were disproportionately endangered by "uncontrolled" toxic-waste sites—i.e., any site specified in the EPA's Comprehensive Environmental Response, Compensation, and Liabilities Information System (CERCLIS)—stating that "three out of every five Black and Hispanic Americans" lived in communities with such sites. But since the 1987 release of the UCC report, the EPA has pronounced 27,000 of what originally were 40,000 "uncontrolled" toxic-waste sites clean or of little or no risk.

No Proof of Injustice

The cry of "environmental racism," buoyed by misleading research, is belied by more careful studies. For example, researchers at the University of Massachusetts based their study not on ZIP Code areas, but on census tracts. Census tracts are both smaller and more definable as neighborhoods than ZIP Code areas. The researchers found that commercial hazardous-waste facilities "are no more likely to be located in tracts with higher percentages of blacks and Hispanics than in other tracts."

In 1992 several partisan EJ papers were published as a group in *The National Law Journal* without prepublication peer review. The articles purported to show racial discrimination in the environmental enforcement process, claiming: (a) that hazardous-waste sites in nonminority communities became members of the National Priorities List of Superfund sites more quickly than did those in minority communities, and (b) that penalties imposed for violations of the Resource Conservation and Recovery Act were lighter in minority communities.

But this study had "serious statistical methodological problems," according to Bernard R. Siskin, Ph.D., a statistician retained by the EPA. These problems included the presentation of statistically insignificant findings. Dr. Siskin ascribed the aforementioned time-lag claim to a "failure . . . to account for the correct date on which the site is first discovered."

Even the GAO, whose 1983 report had provided EJ partisans with ammunition, concluded in a much more elaborate (and widely ignored) 1995 study: "The percentage of minorities and low-income people living within one mile of nonhazardous municipal landfills was more often lower than the percentage in the rest of the country. When the data from our sample were used to make estimates about all nonhazardous municipal landfills in the nation, neither minorities nor low-income people were overrepresented in any consistent manner."

Color Them Egalitarian

Unsettling as the attachment of EJ activists to dubious empirical findings may be, such attachment is not the movement's only serious shortcoming. Another serious, but more subtle, defect is its very nature as a diverse coalition of grassroots groups seeking "redress" of an unlimited number of grievances. For example, Native American activists are often spurred by tribal-culture and sovereignty concerns, while others focus on occupational exposure to chemicals among migrant farmworkers. All such constituencies have been encouraged to vent their claims to the EPA's Office of Environmental Justice (OEJ) and to the National Environmental Justice Advisory Council (NEJAC), the activist-dominated federal advisory committee with which the OEJ closely collaborates.

This diverse "people of color" coalition could not be maintained without faith in the illusion that priorities and tradeoffs are unnecessary. In the world of EJ activism (as in grassroots environmentalism generally), all environmental concerns—childhood lead poisoning, global climate change, nuclear waste, pesticide use, Superfund sites, urban air pollution, and so forth—have equal rank. Of course, prioritization of these concerns would result in neglect of some of them and contention among members of the coalition.

Prioritization of environmental issues is at variance with what makes the EJ movement tick: egalitarianism. In the realm of such activism, the downgrading of any concern amounts to something intolerable to many activists: victimization. The only priority shared by grassroots activists of all ethnicities is citizen involvement. It seems never to have occurred to many activists that the attention they demand for minor, unsubstantiated, or nonexistent problems might distract attention from serious real-life problems, such as lead exposure among urban minority children.

The True Ideals of the EJ Movement

In the final analysis, EJ activism is not a public health movement but a loose aggregation of advocates for grassroots democracy and social justice—including, at an extreme, some who oppose industrial capitalism. Its major political aims include unifying residents and increasing their collective profiles in policy debates and governmental decision-making. Its ultimate aim is to reallocate society's resources. Because of these aims, the movement can ill afford pursuing a health-centered agenda; alleged health hazards that do not readily outrage the public have little utility in mobilizing citizens. Personal danger due to personal behavior—such as smoking—tends not to outrage the public and thus lacks such utility. More useful for mobilization purposes are alleged hazards perceivable as having been imposed on communities by corporations (especially those considered intrusive) or by governmental entities that appear distant, unaccountable, or racist.

An understanding of the fundamental ideals of the EJ movement (and of grassroots environmentalism overall)—democratization and wealth redistribution—facilitates comprehension of the activists' persistent emphasis on such minor or weakly documented hazards as dioxin, environmental "hormone disrupters," or most toxic-waste sites. These ideals also account for the movement's acceptance of intuition as a means of perceiving risk. This is exemplified by the longevity of the thoroughly debunked folklore that the concentration of petrochemical facilities in Louisiana created a "cancer alley."

On the other hand, because smoking is both voluntary and common, tobacco use is not an EJ issue. The approximately 47,000 annual tobacco-related deaths in the African-American community elicit little outrage among EJ activists, partly because these deaths are perceived as proportionate. Even the remarkably high smoking rates among low-income and Native-American citizens provoke little activist concern.

Urban Tobacco Roads

In a change of pace, minority activists tackled a worthy issue in 1990 when R.J. Reynolds Tobacco Company proposed to pitch "Uptown," a then-forthcoming cigarette brand, to the African-American market. This issue had all the elements most useful for mobilizing a community: A distinct, formidable, outside entity explicitly announced that it would target an ethnic group for the marketing of a new and tangible source of harm. Once Secretary of Health and Human Services Louis Sullivan, an African-American, publicly denounced R.J. Reynolds for fostering a "culture of cancer" in the Black community, the company canceled test-marketing of "Uptown."

If only corporations would propose to burn tobacco in urban incinerators, or to bury it in minority-neighborhood landfills. Now *that* would be an environmental justice issue!

Periodical Bibliography

The following articles have been selected to supplement the diverse views presented in this chapter. Addresses are provided for periodicals not indexed in the *Readers' Guide to Periodical Literature*, the *Alternative Press Index*, the *Social Sciences Index*, or the *Index to Legal Periodicals and Books*.

Angie Cannon	"DWB: Driving While Black," *U.S. News & World Report*, March 15, 1999.
David Cole and John Marcello	"Symposium: Is Public Concern About Federal Police Using Racial Profiling Justified?" *Insight*, July 19, 1999. Available from 3600 New York Ave. NE, Washington, DC 20002.
Mary H. Cooper	"Environmental Justice," *CQ Researcher*, June 19, 1998. Available from 1414 22nd St. NW, Washington, DC 20037.
Ellis Cose	"The Good News About Black America," *Newsweek*, June 7, 1999.
Samuel Francis	"Race to a White Minority," *Spectator*, June 28, 1997.
Clyde Haberman	"Cry Racism, and Watch Knees Jerk," *New York Times*, December 4, 1998.
Robin Kelley	"'Yo' Mama's Disfunktional!" *Witness*, March 1998. Available from 7000 Michigan Ave., Detroit, MI 48210-2872.
Mikal Muharrar	"Taking Sides: Differing Media Approaches to the Problem of Racial Profiling," *Extra!* July/August 1999.
Elena Neuman	"*Emerge* and the Lure of Racism," *Weekly Standard*, March 24, 1997. Available from 1211 Avenue of the Americas, New York, NY 10036.
Rebecca Porter	"Skin Deep: Minorities Seek Relief from Racial Profiling," *Trial*, November 1999.
Jason L. Riley	"Don't Cry Wolf on Racism," *Wall Street Journal*, January 26, 1996.
Claude M. Steele	"Thin Ice: 'Stereotype Threat' and Black College Students," *Atlantic Monthly*, August 1999.

CHAPTER 3

How Should Policymakers Respond to Minorities' Concerns?

Chapter Preface

Affirmative action policies were first implemented in the 1960s as a way to correct the effects of discrimination on women and people of color. The government took measures to increase female and minority representation in its workforce and public university populations—typically by including race and gender as factors in hiring and college admissions decisions.

The discrimination that minorities face in the job market is often so subtle and entrenched, affirmative action supporters maintain, that only policies that aggressively seek out minorities can counteract it. According to a 1998 study conducted by the Fair Employment Council, blacks and Latinos encounter discrimination once in every five times they apply for a job. Many whites, on the other hand, have had unfettered access to education and employment due to family ties, school connections, and personal referral networks that minorities are usually not a part of. As a result, claims the Federal Glass Ceiling Commission, 97 percent of senior managers at the top U.S. corporations are white males, yet they make up only 43 percent of the workforce. Preferential hiring of minorities, many contend, is the best way to correct the ongoing injustices that have resulted from decades of preferential hiring of whites.

While most critics of affirmative action commend civil rights laws that ban discrimination against minorities, they argue that the use of any racial preferences is a form of discrimination that thwarts the ideals of equal opportunity and fairness. These critics often contend that less qualified minorities are granted jobs and college admissions at the expense of more qualified whites. In other words, they allege, affirmative action policies give minorities positions largely because of their race and not on the objective basis of merit. The result, critics maintain, is reverse discrimination against whites and the stigmatization of minorities who are seen as needing special treatment to succeed.

Affirmative action is likely to provoke heated debate in the years to come. The following chapter discusses race-based policies and other such issues in greater detail.

> *"The favoritism for certain groups . . . is so strong that it can only be remedied by actively encouraging the promotion of other groups."*

Race Should Be a Consideration in Public Policy

Paul Butler, interviewed by Lloyd Eby

In the following viewpoint, Paul Butler contends that race-based policies such as affirmative action should continue to be on the government's agenda. He maintains that these policies counteract ongoing discrimination against people of color and help to ensure equal opportunity in education and employment. As long as minorities face discrimination because of their skin color, argues Butler, race should be a factor in policymakers' decisions. Butler is a law professor at the George Washington Law School in Washington, D.C. He is interviewed by Lloyd Eby, the assistant senior editor of the monthly news journal *World & I*.

As you read, consider the following questions:

1. According to Butler, what three goals are to be achieved by the use of racial preferences?
2. How does the author respond to the argument that affirmative action stigmatizes people of color?
3. In Butler's opinion, what would be irresponsible about public policies emphasizing "color blindness"?

Excerpted from "Race *Should* Be Used for Governmental Decision Making," by Paul Butler, interviewed by Lloyd Eby. This article appeared in the September 1998 issue of, and is reprinted with permission from, *The World &I*, a publication of The Washington Times Corporation; copyright ©1998.

L loyd Eby: *Professor Butler, do you think it's permissible—legally, ethically, or logically—for government to use race as a criterion for law and policy?*
Paul Butler: It's permissible, desirable, and valuable. The Supreme Court has made it clear—and I agree—that the use of race can at times be good public policy, but not always.
When, for example, would it not be permissible?
I don't think that the way the government used race for most of this country's history is OK. The Jim Crow statutes instituted an American kind of apartheid, with black-only and white-only schools, water fountains, and so on. That is clearly an impermissible use of race.
Where does the law use race outside of affirmative action?
Two examples: It's perfectly permissible in most jurisdictions of the United States for police to consider race in determining whether someone is suspicious—to have a racial profile that says, "Well, gee, if that person's black, then he's more likely to be a drug courier." Another perfectly permissible use of race occurs in prison administration. If, for example, the warden of a prison determines that for disciplinary or other administrative reasons he needs to separate the black prisoners from the Chicano prisoners from the white prisoners, then that's perfectly permissible. These uses of race are upheld by the Supreme Court now, even though they may be very controversial.

The Goal of Race-Based Preferences
What's the goal that you want to achieve with race preferences?
In my writing I've described three different goals. One is to compensate for past discrimination. That is, to put ethnic minorities—and here I'm thinking mainly of African Americans and Native Americans—where they would be, had the discrimination never occurred. That's a classic tort remedy in the law. When someone is injured, when he is deprived in some way by a circumstance that is not his own fault, then the responsible use of the law is to place him where he would be but for the injury. That's one goal of affirmative action—to compensate African Americans for the unimaginable injury of slavery and American apartheid.
The second goal is to compensate for ongoing discrimi-

nation, to achieve equal opportunity. The favoritism for certain groups in the United States is so strong that it can only be remedied by actively encouraging the promotion of other groups. Specifically, favoritism for white people in the United States is such a strong, inviolable part of our country that for African Americans to have a fair chance, they have to be actively considered.

The third goal is diversity, and that's President Bill Clinton's goal when he says he wants a cabinet that looks more like America. That goal of affirmative action is to create a diverse setting, which we in America have always viewed, at least in our rhetoric, as a desirable thing because we understand that our strength comes from diversity.

Now, for whatever reason, we've seen that when race is not considered, when processes are ostensibly color-blind, this often results in environments that are not as diverse or as effective as they could be.

The Stigma Argument

In his memoir Hunger of Memory, *Richard Rodriguez speaks of his experience graduating with a Ph.D. and getting numerous good job offers because he is Hispanic and thus a member of a favored class, while other white colleagues in his class with similar qualifications got no offers or much poorer ones. This is one of the distortions produced by race-based affirmative-action policy.*

This is the classic stigma argument, made by people who oppose fairness preferences. They say affirmative action makes African Americans or white women, or whoever's the beneficiary, feel stigmatized, or makes other people think they got their benefit simply on the basis of race and therefore aren't as qualified.

There are a couple responses to this. The first is that most people who are the beneficiaries of affirmative action do not report feeling this so-called stigma. Relatively few report feeling stigmatized by it, and they are usually opposed to affirmative action for other reasons.

For example, I was admitted to Yale College and Harvard Law School on the basis of affirmative-action programs. I know that to be true because before there was affirmative action at Yale and Harvard Law School, there were very few

African Americans there. Does it mean that black people weren't qualified to attend those institutions? Absolutely not. It's just that for some reason prior to affirmative action those schools didn't admit many African Americans.

The second and most important point is that this stigma argument assumes that the people who are not the beneficiaries of affirmative action are more qualified to be there. In my experience, the quickest way to cure oneself of that belief is to simply interact with your counterparts, particularly your white male counterparts. There is nothing in that experience to suggest that those people are qualified to be there and you're not. So I would have recommended that Rodriguez just accept one of those opportunities and then look at the people, the white men in particular, who got in those positions outside of affirmative action. I don't think that he would have felt less qualified and believed that they were more qualified.

Again, we certainly know that people get opportunities, especially to teach at a college, on the basis of all kinds of criteria.

The Problem with "Color-Blindness"

I think we should want to move toward a situation in which race is a nullity, where it doesn't matter. Would you agree with that?

Not necessarily. The idea of color-blindness as a value is relatively new, and it's certainly controversial. We've never been color-blind, never had a color-blind society, and we really only started talking about it as an important value in [the twentieth] century, when African Americans and other ethnic minorities started asking for equal rights.

This legal notion of color-blindness first appears in the law in Justice John Marshall Harlan's opinion, writing in dissent in the *Plessy v. Ferguson* case. There for the first time Justice Harlan proclaimed that the U.S. Constitution demands color-blindness, which in and of itself was a radical and very new proposition. But then he goes on to say that the white race is the dominant race in the United States, and so it will always be. He says color-blindness is not a threat to the dominance of the white race. Thus, the idea of color-blindness is born.

I think time has proven Justice Harlan correct. That is, that now, in an era ostensibly of equality for African Americans and other ethnic minorities, if the law and public policy are color-blind, this will result in the continued dominance of the white race. Given the history of the United States, color-blindness is the equivalent of white supremacy. This is because you can't have three hundred years of law and public policy all designed to subordinate a group—to be actively hostile to them—and then say, "Hey, everything's hunky-dory. Now we're going to be color-blind. Pull yourself up by your own bootstraps." That's irresponsible law. It's irresponsible public policy, and moreover, it doesn't work.

Bruce Beattie. Reprinted by permission of Copley News Service.

In what sense does it not work?

Take Thurgood Marshall's famous example of staging a race and holding one person back for miles and then saying, "OK, let's start the race now." Of course the other guy is already way ahead, even at the beginning of the race, and that's just not fair. That's what the law has done to African Americans and some other ethnic minorities in the United States. It's held them back for literally hundreds of years, and the color-blind argument, or the anti-affirmative-action argument, says, "OK, now you're ready to start the race. Everybody start in your own place." That is simply not fair.

But if you take that view, haven't you set up a form of public racism in perpetuity because you instantiate the notion of some sort of racial consciousness?

I don't think that race consciousness is at all the same as racism. In fact, it's a somewhat absurd idea in my mind. I can't think of any other context in which it's desirable to be blind. We usually think of people who are blind as being handicapped. So it's something of a bizarre notion that all of a sudden we want our law and our public policy to be blind to one of the fundamental realities in the United States, which is that race matters.

But we do accept the principle that law and public policy ought to be blind with respect to religious differences.

Well, not necessarily. Again, our public policy says that the law should not respect any one particular religion, but we don't expect our law and public policy to act like religion doesn't exist. That's what the anti-affirmative-action agenda is: to pretend as though race doesn't exist.

Rancor Between the Races

If you accept this notion that race ought to be a component or a criterion for judgment, can race be used in any noninvidious way— that is, without increasing the level of rancor?

I think that, first of all, when you talk about increasing the level of rancor, you should understand that rancor exists with and without affirmative action.

On that point I agree, but the question is, Are we making it worse, or making it better?

Well, it depends on whose rancor you're talking about. If you're talking about the proverbial angry white men, I guess in a sense you're making them even angrier when you use affirmative action. But when you talk about rancor, it's very interesting to see what kind of issues have caused rancor between the races in the United States.

Some people make what I call the backlash argument, insisting that proponents of affirmative action should not ask for what they believe to be responsible public policy because that would create white backlash. But the fact is that almost any demand—in fact, every demand that I can think of for civil rights by African Americans—has caused white backlash.

When I think of the most troublesome contemporaneous image of white supremacy that I encountered as a young person, it was the famous picture in the *Boston Globe* of the African-American man being stabbed by an unruly white mob, and the instrument that they were using to stab him was the American flag. When I saw that picture, I wondered, What could this man have done to provoke that kind of anger?

What he had done was to demand that the children of Boston attend integrated schools. When we look at the last fifty years, what has caused the most white anger and backlash has been the demand for African-American schoolchildren to go to integrated schools. So if your argument is that fear of backlash should limit the demands or aspirations of African Americans, then African Americans shouldn't advocate affirmative action. But we also should not advocate integrated schools, or equal opportunity in the workplace, or any of the other demands we have made in the past hundred years in the face of constant and uniform rancor, anger, and backlash.

The fact is that if African Americans allow the threat of white backlash to moderate their political and legal aspirations, they would scarcely progress at all.

Defining Race

What about the problem of definition for race? As you know, there's a census . . . in the year 2000, and they're coping with the problem of how to define members of various races for the purpose of census enumeration.

To take a personal example, I have a colleague who is British and his wife is Korean. I have another acquaintance, a lawyer, who is a white Canadian and his wife is a light-skinned black person from Texas with some American Indian in her ancestry. Both couples have children. Suppose these children were to intermarry and have children. What race would the grandchildren be?

It seems to me that race is a plastic, malleable quality; it's not fixed.

Right. It's not biological. It's a social construct, that's true. But nonetheless, social constructs are real, even if they're not biological.

Then how do we define them?

We set criteria that on some level we understand are going to be arbitrary. But the law does that. Every time the law constructs a definition, it's almost inevitably arbitrary, and we understand that.

I was reading a law review article that raises the issue you've raised. A whole conference was devoted to this idea of race being a social construct, which again, is certainly true. Then these three men, who before the conference had described themselves as black, left the conference convinced that race doesn't really exist, because it's really composed of all these arbitrary categories.

They went to the streets to go to a restaurant to celebrate their newfound understanding of race, and they couldn't get a cab because the cabdrivers in the city perceived them as black, and black people have a tough time getting cabs in most big cities. It's ironic that here we've decided that race doesn't exist, or that it's hard to categorize, but people who want to use it as a criterion don't seem to have much of a problem.

These men perceived themselves as black before they went to this high fallutin' conference that decided blackness wasn't real. But then on the street no one had much of a problem deciding they were black. And in fact, when we think of the ways that it's permissible outside of affirmative action for the law to use race now, there are very few discussions or critiques of those laws on the basis of race being a hard-to-define category.

It seems to me that the methods here thwart the goals. In other words, implementing any program for race-based governmental action is in fact racist because it involves the reification of race.

So it's racist to understand that race exists and that race matters?

Yes. It seems to me that it is.

No, that's absurd. It's like saying it's racist to see a tree and call it a tree.

No, trees we know about. Trees are definable.

And race and racism are definable as well.

So what you've done is made race a fixed and ineliminable category of human affairs.

I don't know what you mean by a fixed and ineliminatable

category. I would hope that we're not trying to eliminate race, since race matters. That's scary. That sounds like a final solution to me. I think if you asked Hitler how you get rid of anti-Semitism, he would have said, "That's what I'm trying to do." So I think that acting like race doesn't matter will eliminate race—that's a frightening concept.

Why Does Race Matter?

I still think the goal we—human beings in general—should want is a situation in which race does not matter.

Human beings are a very diverse bunch of people, and they don't all want the same thing. The "we" who don't want race to matter now are the people who will benefit from ostensible color-blindness. Again, those are the people who started the game way, way ahead because of rules that they made. So of course, if those people are not concerned about their fellow Americans, it's in their very pecuniary interest to want race not to exist. They pretend, like all of a sudden, after race existed with a vengeance for three hundred years, that now it doesn't exist anymore.

If that's the "we" you're talking about, then yes, those people don't want race to *exist* anymore. But why is it desirable to be blind? Why is it a good public policy to act like something that matters with a vengeance doesn't matter?

Being discriminated against because of how you look is a deficiency.

Yes, I agree completely on that point.

So it needs to be compensated.

And you don't agree that the process of compensation is belying our goal, the goal where we seek to be human apart from race?

Again, I don't know who has that goal. We see human beings as human including their race. We won't be seeing human beings—we won't be truly seeing—if we're partially blind. That's the irony of the color-blind debate. How can we see if we're blind?

"Racial-preference policies may provide some blacks with material benefits, but they will never promote genuine progress."

Race Should Not Be a Consideration in Public Policy

Part I: Gerald Reynolds; Part II: Charles T. Canady

Racial-preference policies are counterproductive, contend the authors of the following two-part viewpoint. In Part I, Gerald Reynolds argues that racial preferences often grant rewards to underqualified minorities and ultimately work against minority progress. Reynolds, an attorney, is a senior fellow at the Center for New Black Leadership in Washington, D.C. In Part II, Florida Republican representative Charles T. Canady contends that racial preferences are a form of government-imposed discrimination that should be abandoned. He maintains that the purpose of preferences was to eliminate the effects of racism, but they have served only to emphasize racial distinctions and intensify racial divisiveness.

As you read, consider the following questions:

1. In Reynolds's opinion, what factors stand in the way of black progress?
2. How did Hubert Humphrey, quoted by Canady, define discrimination?
3. In what way does the system of racial preferences harm its supposed beneficiaries, in Canady's opinion?

Part I: Excerpted from "Government Is a Barrier to Progress," by Gerald Reynolds. This article appeared in the February 1999 issue of, and is reprinted with permission from, *The World & I,* a publication of The Washington Times Corporation; copyright ©1999. *Part II:* Reprinted with permission from *Insight* magazine from "Q: Should Washington End All Preferences in Hiring and Contracting? Yes: Discriminatory Preferential Treatment Undermines Fundamental American Ideals," by Charles T. Canady, *Insight,* April 27, 1998. Copyright 1998 News World Communications, Inc. All rights reserved.

I

Traditional civil rights organizations, such as the National Association for the Advancement of Colored People, deserve a great deal of praise for advancing freedom on behalf of black Americans. Prior to the civil rights revolution, virulent racism combined with state-sponsored discrimination constituted insurmountable barriers to progress for most blacks.

A black's political, economic, and social status in life was not determined by drive, industry, initiative, and intellect. Much like the status-based societies of eighteenth-century Europe, American society established barriers that made it virtually impossible for blacks to significantly improve their well-being.

It was the traditional civil rights groups with their winning strategies that eliminated de jure discrimination and precipitated a sea change in the racial attitudes of most white Americans. Instead of recognizing the new challenges that blacks face, however, these groups have been clinging to their outdated concepts.

What Hinders Black Progress?

The key to understanding the decline of traditional civil rights organizations and the growing stature of black conservatives is the ability and willingness to assess the problems confronting black Americans with precision. Since the founding of the Republic, it was clear that virulent racism and southern-style apartheid were absolute barriers to progress for most blacks.

However, this is no longer the case. Now a confluence of factors—such as crime, substandard academic performance, and out-of-wedlock births—stands in the way of progress.

Rather than promote public-policy prescriptions that address these problems, traditional civil rights groups have merely used these social problems to extract benefits from the government and corporate America via racial-preference policies. Two of the most salient differences between traditional civil rights advocates and black conservatives—who are best represented by Supreme Court Justice Clarence Thomas, California Supreme Court Associate Justice Janice

116

Rogers Brown, and scholar Thomas Sowell—are the latter's (1) principled objection to the government's use of race-based affirmative-action policies and (2) willingness to promote policies that increase the productive capacity of disadvantaged blacks.

Race-Based Affirmative Action

At the turn of the [twentieth] century, black sharecroppers, as well as black scholars, knew that blacks had to be twice as good as their white competitors to be considered for a contract, job, or seat at a college. Blacks knew that they had to exceed the prescribed standard. Many black conservatives believe that genuine progress depends on meeting or exceeding real-world standards.

Rather than provide blacks with the skills and values needed to meet or exceed real-world standards, civil rights groups promote policies that lower the bar for blacks. They support a dual system. One demands that whites and Asians meet rigorous standards. The other demands that blacks and Hispanics meet standards that are less rigorous. Racial-preference policies may provide some blacks with material benefits, but they will never promote genuine progress.

On the surface, those who argue that racial-preference policies are needed to remedy the lingering effects of slavery and invidious discrimination make a compelling argument. However, upon closer examination, one discovers the argument's fatal flaws.

Race-based affirmative action has little to do with remedying the effects of slavery and virulent forms of racism. I'd like to suggest that the primary legacy of our history of oppression is a set of behavioral patterns. The degree to which these patterns are distributed among the black population varies. This explains the divergent trend lines in the black community.

Generally, those blacks who possess a strong work ethic, take full advantage of their educational opportunities, refrain from having children out-of-wedlock, and obey the law are propelled into the middle class and beyond. On the other side, those blacks who lack "middle class" values are precluded from any chance of advancement.

The Importance of Human Capital

Although the attributes and habits of mind needed to climb the socioeconomic ladder are often referred to as "middle class" values, economists refer to this bundle of values as human or social capital. Since the beginning of time, the most efficient method of transferring social capital was through the family. The government can transmit human capital by supporting a system that rewards those who meet the prescribed standard and withholds rewards from those who fail to meet this standard. This system creates incentives and disincentives that shape behavior.

To give an individual who has failed to meet a prescribed standard the same reward received by an individual who has met or exceeded the standard reduces the former's incentive to work harder. No economist worth his salt would dispute this as a general proposition. The eminent scholars Thomas Sowell and Gary Becker have written on the importance of human capital and how incentives shape behavior.

Although most black conservatives are not trained economists, many instinctively grasp the fact that policies that lower the bar for blacks act as "headwinds" blowing against genuine black progress. This is not to say that blacks do not profit from racial-preference policies. What blacks receive from these policies are material benefits, such as a seat in an elite university or a set-aside contract.

However, racial-preference policies do not increase the productive capacity of their beneficiaries. This type of dependence is the antithesis of freedom. Unless blacks have the values and skills needed to acquire material benefits without government intervention, they will forever depend on the kindness of strangers. Unlike Jesse Jackson and other members of the civil rights establishment, black conservatives seek to push those blacks who lack sufficient human capital toward freedom.

The ultimate burden of advancing the interest of black Americans rests with black Americans, not the government. While many civil rights advocates will readily agree with this proposition, their singular pursuit of policies that place the burden of black progress in the hands of government bureaucrats belies their public pronouncements to the contrary. This is not to say that blacks should not form alliances with third parties to promote their interests. I am suggesting we test policies by asking this simple question: Is the proposed policy likely to increase the productive capacity of its beneficiaries?

II

The American people are debating the use of race and gender preferences by federal, state and local governments. In 1996, a majority of voters in California, including 29 percent of blacks, approved the California Civil Rights Initiative prohibiting preferential treatment in public employment, education and contracting. In November 1998, voters in Washington state will consider a referendum to end the use of race and gender preferences by state and local governments. [This referendum passed.] In a series of cases, the Supreme Court and federal courts of appeal have made it clear that the system of preference is built on an exceedingly shaky foundation. These cases—chiefly the *Adarand vs. Peña* decision of 1995—establish that racial classifications are presumptively unconstitutional and will be permitted only in extraordinary circumstances.

Racial preferences are fundamentally inconsistent with our most deeply cherished principles. The ideal of respect for the dignity of the individual was set forth in the Declaration of Independence: "[A]ll men are created equal" and are "endowed by their Creator with certain unalienable rights." At Independence Hall on the eve of the Civil War, Abraham Lincoln spoke of this ideal as "a great principle or idea" in the Declaration of Independence "which gave promise that in due time the weights should be lifted from the shoulders of all men, and that all should have an equal chance." This ideal undergirded the historic civil-rights movement and condemned the contradictions of the American system of segregation.

No one expressed this idea more eloquently than the Rev. Martin Luther King Jr., who said, the "image of God . . . is universally shared in equal portions by all men. There is no graded scale of essential worth. Every human being has etched in his personality the indelible stamp of the Creator.

. . . The worth of an individual does not lie in the measure of his intellect, his racial origin or his social position. Human worth lies in relatedness to God." King's view propelled the civil-rights movement to great victories.

The Principle of Colorblind Justice

The principle of colorblind justice ultimately found clear expression in the law of the United States. With the adoption of the Civil Rights Act of 1964, the Congress acted decisively against the Jim Crow system and established a national policy against discrimination based on race and sex. It is the supreme irony of the modern civil-rights movement that this crowning achievement soon was followed by the creation of a system of preferences based first on race and then extended to gender.

The Civil Rights Act of 1964 constituted an unequivocal statement that Americans should be treated as individuals and not as members of racial and gender groups. Under the Civil Rights Act of 1964, no American would be subject to discrimination. And there was no question about what "discrimination" meant. Hubert Humphrey—the chief Senate sponsor of the legislation—stated it as clearly as possible: Discrimination was any "distinction in treatment given to different individuals because of their different race."

While considering the Civil Rights Act of 1964, Congress debated the issues of racial preferences and proportional representation. The product of that debate was the adoption of Section 703(j) of the act, which states that nothing in Title VII of the act "shall be interpreted to require any employer . . . to grant preferential treatment to any individual or group because of the race . . . of such individual or group" to maintain a racial balance.

In violation of the clear policy established by the Civil Rights Act of 1964, discrimination of a most flagrant kind now is practiced at the federal, state and local government levels. A white teacher in Piscataway, N.J., is fired solely on account of her race. Asian students are denied admission to state universities to make room for students of other races with much weaker academic records. There are more than 160 federal laws, regulations and executive orders explicitly requiring race- and sex-based preferences.

Who Benefits from Preferences?

Racial preferences frequently are justified as a measure to help low-income blacks. But the evidence is compelling that the beneficiaries of preferential policies overwhelmingly are middle class or wealthy. For the most part, the truly disadvantaged have been unable to participate in the programs that grant preferences. Furthermore, the emphasis on preferences has diverted attention from the task of addressing the root causes of black Americans' disadvantage. The lagging educational achievement of disadvantaged blacks can be ameliorated not through preferences but through structural reform of the American elementary and secondary education system. Preferences do nothing to help develop the skills necessary for the economic and social advancement of the disadvantaged.

Although some individuals have benefited from preferences, and a case can be made that the economic position of the black middle class has been enhanced by preferences, these gains have come at a great moral cost. Put simply, preferences discriminate. They result in individuals being denied opportunities solely because they are members of a certain race, gender or ethnic group. The ambitions and aspirations, the hopes and the dreams of individual Americans for themselves and for their families are trampled underfoot not for any wrongs those individuals have committed but for the sake of a bureaucratic effort to counterbalance the putative racism of American society. The penalty for the supposed sins of the society at large is imposed on individuals who themselves are guilty only of being born a member of a nonpreferred group. Individual American citizens who otherwise would enjoy jobs and other opportunities are told that they must be denied to adjust the scales of racial justice.

Although preferences are presented as a remedial measure, they in fact create a class of innocent victims of intentional government-imposed discrimination. In our system of justice, the burden of a remedy is imposed on those who are responsible for the specific harm that is being remedied. In the case of racial preferences, however, this remedial model breaks down. Those who benefit from the remedy need not show that they have in fact suffered any harm, and those who bear the burden of the remedy do so not because of any conduct on their part but purely because of their identity as members of nonpreferred groups. Americans of all descriptions are deprived of opportunities under the system of preferences. And many of these victims have themselves struggled to overcome a severely disadvantaged background.

Affirmative Action Versus Equal Rights

We need to have and enforce civil rights laws that bar discrimination on the basis of color. The problem is that many people equate antidiscrimination laws with affirmative action programs. They are, in fact, opposites.

True civil rights, including antidiscrimination laws, are colorblind. Affirmative action, on the other hand, specifically uses race and ethnicity as the basis for special treatment regarding contracts, hiring, or admissions. The difference is this: Equal rights opens doors regardless of race, while affirmative action "opens doors" because of race. In my view, they are diametrically opposed.

Armstrong Williams, *World & I*, June 1998.

Proponents of preferential policies must face the reality of the injuries perpetrated on innocent individuals and confront the undeniable facts concerning the daily operation of the system of preferences in awarding contracts, jobs, promotions and other opportunities. The reality of preferences is hidden beneath a facade of "plus factors, goals and timetables" and other measures said merely to "open up access" to opportunities. Behind all the semantic games played under the banner of affirmative action are the lives of individual Americans who are denied opportunities by government simply because they are of the wrong color or sex. The names assigned to the policies that deprive them of opportunity are of little moment. What matters is that our government implements a broad range of programs with the purpose of granting favored treatment to some on the basis of their biological characteristics.

Attacking the Dignity of Minorities

The moral failure of preferences extends beyond the injustice done to individuals who are denied opportunities because they belong to the wrong group. There are other victims of the system of preferences. The supposed beneficiaries are themselves victims.

Preferences attack the dignity of the preferred and cast a pall of doubt over their competence and worth. Preferences send a message that those in the favored groups are deemed incapable of meeting the standards that others are required to meet. Simply because they are members of a preferred group, individuals often are deprived of the recognition and respect they have earned. The achievements gained through talent and hard work are attributed instead to the operation of the system of preferences. The abilities of the preferred are called into question not only in the eyes of the society at large but also in the eyes of the preferred themselves. Self-confidence is eroded, standards are lowered, incentives to perform are diminished and pernicious stereotypes are reinforced.

All of this results from treating individuals on the basis of their race. It is the inevitable consequence of reducing individuals to the status of racial entities. The lesson of our history as Americans is that racial distinctions are inherently cruel. Although the purpose underlying preferences was to eliminate the vestiges of racism, the mechanism chosen to accomplish that purpose was fundamentally flawed. Rather than breaking down racial barriers, preferential policies consistently remind Americans of racial differences.

Congress must act now to end these destructive and harmful preferences. At the same time, we must support affirmative outreach and recruitment efforts to ensure that all segments of society are aware of opportunities. We should reach out and bring people into the pool of applicants for opportunities, but no one should be granted or denied an opportunity because of his or her race or gender. Everyone should be treated without regard to race or gender as an individual who is equal in the eyes of the law.

"If universities were flatly prohibited from consideting race in admissions . . . over half of the black students in selective colleges today would have been rejected."

Colleges Should Use Race-Sensitive Admissions Policies

William G. Bowen and Derek Bok

Former Princeton University president William G. Bowen and former Harvard University president Derek Bok are the authors of *The Shape of the River: Long-Term Consequences of Considering Race in College and University Admissions.* In the following viewpoint, Bowen and Bok argue that race-sensitive admissions policies have benifited both minority and white college students. Their survey of thousands of students from selective colleges and universities indicates that most blacks admitted under affirmative action policies pursued successful careers after graduating. Moreover, they contend, race-sensitive policies help to create a healthy and diverse learning environment that enriches all college students.

As you read, consider the following questions:

1. In the opinion of Bowen and Bok, why did colleges and universities start considering race in their admissions policies?
2. What is the average income of the surveyed black male college graduates who entered selective schools in 1976, according to the authors?
3. According to Bowen and Bok, why do selective colleges sometimes reject students who graduated at the top of their high school class?

Reprinted, with permission, from "The Proof Is in the Pudding," by William G. Bowen and Derek Bok, *The Washington Post National Weekly Edition*, September 28, 1998.

In his classic 1969 study of Wall Street lawyers, Erwin Smigel reported that: "I only heard of three Negroes who had been hired by large law firms. Two of these were women who did not meet the client." Smigel's statement should not surprise us. In the 1960s, barely 2 percent of America's doctors and lawyers were black, and only 280 blacks held elected office of any kind. At that time, few leading professional schools and nationally prominent colleges and universities enrolled more than a handful of blacks. Late in the decade, however, selective institutions set about to change these statistics, not by establishing quotas, but by considering race, along with many other factors, in deciding whom to admit.

This policy was adopted because of a widely shared conviction that it was simply wrong for overwhelming numbers of blacks to continue to hold routine jobs while the more influential positions were almost always held by whites. In a nation becoming more racially and ethnically diverse, these educators also considered it vital to create a learning environment that would prepare students of all races to live and work together effectively.

The Results of Race-Based Policies

In recent years, the use of race in college admissions has been vigorously contested in several states and in the courts. In 1996, a federal appeals court in New Orleans, deciding the *Hopwood vs. Texas* case, declared such a race-sensitive policy unconstitutional when its primary aim is not to remedy some specific wrong from the past. Californians have voted to ban all consideration of race in admitting students to public universities. Surprisingly, however, amid much passionate debate, there has been little hard evidence of how these policies work and what their consequences have been.

To remedy this deficiency, we examined the college and later-life experiences of more than 35,000 students—almost 3,000 of whom were black—who had entered 28 selective colleges and universities in the fall of 1976 and the fall of 1989. This massive database, built jointly by the schools and the Andrew W. Mellon Foundation, for the first time links information such as SAT scores and college majors to experiences after college, including graduate and professional degrees, earnings and civic involvement. Most of our study focused on African Americans and whites, because the Latino population at these schools was too small to permit the same sort of analysis. What did we discover?

Compared with their extremely high-achieving white classmates, black students in general received somewhat lower college grades and graduated at moderately lower rates. The reasons for these disparities are not fully understood, and selective institutions need to be more creative in helping improve black performance, as a few universities already have succeeded in doing. Still, 75 percent graduated within six years, a figure well above the 40 percent of blacks and 59 percent of whites who graduated nationwide from the 305 universities tracked by the National Collegiate Athletic Association. Moreover, blacks did not earn degrees from these selective schools by majoring in easy subjects. They chose substantially the same concentrations as whites and were just as likely to have difficult majors, such as those in the sciences.

The Success of Black Graduates

Although more than half of the black students attending these schools would have been rejected under a race-neutral admissions regime—that is, if only high school grades and test scores had been counted—they have done exceedingly well after college. Fifty-six percent of the black graduates who had entered these selective schools in 1976 went on to earn advanced degrees. A remarkable 40 percent received either PhDs or professional degrees in the most sought-after fields of law, business and medicine, a figure slightly higher than that for their white classmates and five times higher than that for blacks with bachelor's degrees nationwide. (As a measure of change, it is worth noting that by 1995, 7.5 percent of all law students in the United States were black, up from barely 1 percent in 1960; and 8.1 percent of medical school students were black, compared with 2.2 percent in the mid-1960s. Black elected officials now number more than 8,600.)

By the time of our survey, black male graduates who had entered selective schools in 1976 were earning an average of

$85,000 a year, 82 percent more than other black male college graduates nationwide. Their black female classmates earned 73 percent more than all black women with bachelor's degrees. Not only has the marketplace valued the work of these graduates highly, but the premium associated with attending one of these selective institutions was substantial. Overall, we found that among blacks with similar test scores, the more selective the college they attended, the more likely they were to graduate, earn advanced degrees and receive high salaries. This was generally true for whites as well.

Despite their high salaries, the blacks in our study were not just concerned with their own advancement. In virtually every type of civic activity, from social service organizations to parent-teacher associations, black men were more likely than their white classmates to hold leadership positions. Much the same pattern holds for women. These findings should reassure black intellectuals who have worried that blacks—especially black men—would ignore their social responsibilities once they achieved financial success.

Satisfaction with College

Were black students demoralized by having to compete with whites with higher high school grades and test scores? Is it true, as Dinesh D'Souza asserts in his book *Illiberal Education*, that "American universities are quite willing to sacrifice the future happiness of many young blacks and Hispanics to achieve diversity, proportional representation, and what they consider to be multicultural progress"? The facts are very clear on this point. Far from being demoralized, blacks from the most competitive schools are the most satisfied with their college experience. More than 90 percent of both blacks and whites in our survey said they were satisfied or very satisfied with their college experience, and blacks were even more inclined than whites to credit their undergraduate experience with helping them learn crucial skills. We found no evidence that significant numbers of blacks felt stigmatized by race-sensitive policies. Only 7 percent of black graduates said they would not attend the same selective college if they had to choose again.

Former students of all races reported feeling that learning

to live and work effectively with members of other races is important. Large majorities also believed that their college experience contributed a lot in this respect. Consequently, almost 80 percent of the white graduates favored either retaining the current emphasis on enrolling a diverse class or emphasizing it more. Their minority classmates supported these policies even more strongly.

Arguments Against Racial Considerations Lack Substance

In *The Shape of the River*, William Bowen and Derek Bok analyze data on more than 80,000 students who entered eleven colleges and seventeen universities in 1951, 1976, and 1989, 45,000 of them in the latter two years. The data are eye-opening. To cite one example: Among approximately 700 blacks who matriculated at the schools in 1976, but who likely would have been denied admission under entirely race-neutral admissions policies, more than 225 attained professional degrees or doctorates; nearly 125 are business executives; and over 300 are active in civic life. The data led Bowen and Bok to observe that "[o]n inspection, many of the arguments against considering race in admissions—such as allegations of unintended harm to the intended beneficiaries and enhanced racial tensions on campus—seem to us to lack substance."

Martin Michaelson, *National Forum*, Winter 1999.

Some critics allege that race-sensitive admissions policies aggravate racial tensions by creating resentment among white and Asian students rejected by colleges they hoped to attend. Although we could not test this possibility definitively, we did examine the feelings of white students in our sample who had been rejected by their first-choice school. Significantly, they said they supported an emphasis on diversity just as strongly as students who got into their first-choice schools.

The Misunderstood Concept of Merit

Our findings also clarify the much misunderstood concept of merit in college admission. Many people suppose that all students with especially high grades and test scores "deserve" to be admitted and that it is unfair to reject them in favor of minority applicants with lower grades and test scores. But selective colleges do not automatically offer admission as a reward for past performance to anyone. Nor should they. For any institution, choosing fairly, "on the merits," means selecting applicants by criteria that are reasonably related to the purposes of the organization. For colleges and universities, this means choosing academically qualified applicants who not only give promise of earning high grades but who also can enlarge the understanding of other students and contribute after graduation to their professions and communities. Though clearly relevant, grades and test scores are by no means all that matter.

Because other factors are important—including hard-to-quantify attributes such as determination, motivation, creativity and character—many talented students, white and black, are rejected even though they finished in the top 5 percent of their high school class. The applicants selected are students who were also above a high academic threshold but who seemed to have a greater chance of enhancing the education of their classmates and making a substantial contribution to their professions and society. Seen from the perspective of how well they served the missions of these educational institutions, the students admitted were surely "meritorious."

Achieving Diversity

Could the values of diversity be achieved equally well without considering race explicitly? The Texas legislature has tried to do so by guaranteeing admission to the state's public universities for all students who finish in the top 10 percent of their high school class. Others have suggested using income rather than race to achieve diversity. Our analysis indicates that neither alternative is likely to be as effective as race-sensitive admissions in enrolling an academically well prepared and diverse student body. The Texas approach would admit some students from weaker high schools while turning down better-prepared applicants who happen not to finish in the top tenth of their class in academically stronger schools. Income-based strategies are unlikely to be good substitutes for race-sensitive admissions policies because there are simply too few blacks and Latinos from poor families who have strong enough academic records to qualify for admission to highly selective institutions.

What would happen if universities were flatly prohibited from considering race in admissions? Our findings suggest that over half of the black students in selective colleges today would have been rejected. We can estimate what would be lost as a result:

Of the more than 700 black students who would have been rejected in 1976 under a race-neutral standard, more than 225 went on to earn doctorates or degrees in law, medicine or business. Approximately 70 are now doctors and roughly 60 are lawyers. Almost 125 are business executives. The average earnings of all 700 exceeds $71,000, and well over 300 are leaders of civic organizations.

The impact of race-neutral admissions would be especially drastic in admission to professional schools. The proportion of black students in the Top Ten law, business and medical schools would probably decline to less than 1 percent. These are the main professional schools from which most leading hospitals, law firms and corporations recruit. The result of race-neutral admissions, therefore, would be to damage severely the prospects for developing a larger minority presence in the corporate and professional leadership of America.

The ultimate issue in considering race-sensitive admissions policies is how the country can best prepare itself for a society in which one-third of the population will be black and Latino by the time today's college students are at the height of their careers. With that in mind, would it be wise to reduce substantially the number of well-prepared blacks and Latinos graduating from many of our leading colleges and professional schools?

Considering students' own views about what they have gained from living and learning with classmates from different backgrounds and races, and the demonstrated success of black graduates in the workplace and the community, we do not think so.

*"Does it really make sense to offer
preferences for slots in medical school
because young black men have a harder
time hailing a cab?"*

Colleges Should Not Use Race-Sensitive Admissions Policies

Roger Clegg

In the following viewpoint, Roger Clegg maintains that the use of race-based affirmative action in college admissions is counterproductive. For one thing, he contends, racial preferences unfairly discriminate against students who had nothing to do with any prejudice experienced by the minority students being favored. Moreover, the practice of admitting less-qualified minorities to schools compromises educational standards; it also creates resentment among nonminority students and minimizes the achievements of blacks and Hispanics who do not need special treatment to get admitted to college. Clegg is vice president and general counsel of the Center for Equal Opportunity, a Washington, D.C.–based think tank.

As you read, consider the following questions:

1. According to Clegg, what are the three kinds of arguments typically used by those who support racial preferences in higher education?
2. In the author's opinion, what is flawed about the argument that affirmative action redresses past discrimination?
3. Why is racial diversity not a suitable rationale for upholding race-based admissions policies, in Clegg's opinion?

Excerpted from "Racial and Ethnic Preferences in Higher Education," by Roger Clegg, *National Forum: The Phi Kappa Phi Journal*, vol. 79, no. 1 (Winter 1999). Copyright by Roger Clegg. Reprinted by permission of the publishers.

An important question in higher education today is whether colleges should discriminate in admissions on the basis of race or ethnicity. In framing the issue of "affirmative action" in these terms, I do not mean to suggest that the answer has to be no, but we do have to be honest in admitting that this is the issue.

Those favoring discrimination often avoid this honesty. If accused of advocating discrimination, they will respond, for instance, by saying that race or ethnicity is "only one factor among many that should be considered." But that still means that there will be some cases—in fact, as a series of studies by the Center for Equal Opportunity has shown, this "one factor" is very often given heavy weight—in which it makes the difference between whether someone is admitted to a college or not. If that is not true, then why consider race or ethnicity at all? And when it is true, then discrimination has occurred.

Defenders of preferences also will frequently point out that the SAT is not a perfect predictor of future performance at college and that other admission criteria frequently used—like being a good tennis player or the offspring of an alumnus—are even less predictive. If schools are using selection devices that are defective for whatever reason, go ahead and criticize them, but do not think for a minute that such criticisms make considerations of race and ethnicity any less discriminatory.

So, we are dealing with discrimination—the real question is, Is the discrimination worth it? To answer that, we must consider both the purported benefits and the costs of preferences.

The claimed benefits for the use of preferences fall into three categories: prophylactic, remedial, and diversity. The prophylactic justification is that we must affirmatively discriminate in favor of a group's members lest we fall into discriminating against them. The remedial justification is that discrimination now in favor of members of a group can help make up for discrimination in the past against members of that group. And the diversity rationale is that there are benefits to having certain groups represented at the school.

The Prophylactic Argument

The prophylactic argument has very little plausibility in American higher education today. Do we really need preferences to keep college admission officers from discriminating against blacks and Hispanics? Of course not: the only discrimination they are apparently inclined toward is against whites and Asians. It is sometimes argued that, even if admission officers will not discriminate, others in society will. But does it really make sense to offer preferences for slots in medical school because young black men have a harder time hailing a cab? The Supreme Court has repeatedly dismissed such an untethered rationale.

The Remedial Argument

There is also an obvious pitfall with the second, remedial rationale: discrimination in favor of today's individuals in group X does nothing to help the different individuals in group X who suffered discrimination in the past. The justification, then, must argue that the very individuals who suffered discrimination against them are the ones who now will be receiving discrimination in their favor, or that the discrimination suffered in the past has had discriminatory results still being felt by those in group X.

As to the first justification, bear in mind that, in the context of college admissions, we are dealing mostly with eighteen-year-olds, born in the 1980s. They probably have not participated much in the work force; if they have, the laws prohibiting discrimination against them on the basis of race or ethnicity have been in effect since long before they were born. Nor have they suffered discrimination in education. Public schools are no longer segregated by race or ethnicity, nor are most private schools.

There are exceptions to the statements in the preceding paragraph. Some eighteen-year-olds may have suffered employment discrimination because of their race or ethnicity; some public schools may receive less funding because of the ethnicity of the children who go there; maybe some students are not pressed as hard because of their skin color. But the point is that an eighteen-year-old today is unlikely to have suffered the kind of systematic discrimination against him or her that would justify systematic discrimination in his or her favor.

So, under the remedial rationale, we are left to consider preferences for race and ethnicity because of the historical effects of discrimination being felt by the descendants of those who suffered the discrimination firsthand. Whether such preferences make sense will hinge on how good a "fit" there is between the class of people who have a particular color or ethnicity and the class of people who are suffering because of past discrimination against their ancestors.

A Poor Fit

The fit is a poor one. There are, to mix a metaphor, too many false negatives and too many false positives. That is, many people who are descended from past sufferers of discrimination are *not* eligible for preferences, and many who are not so descended *will* be eligible. For instance, not only blacks and Hispanics but also Jews, Asians, American Indians, and Americans of Irish, Italian, Polish, and German origin have all been subjected to discrimination at one time or another in this country. Conversely, some blacks are descendants of recent immigrants and can hardly claim to have suffered even indirectly from slavery and the Jim Crow laws; a high percentage of Hispanics are immigrants or descended from recent immigrants. It is also unclear why the only relevant discrimination to consider is that which occurred in the United States. If a college wants to right the wrongs of past discrimination that it did not itself commit, then why does it matter where the discrimination occurred? This really would open the floodgates, because many, many immigrants—especially the early WASPs, whose descendants everyone hates—were fleeing religious or some other kind of persecution in their native countries.

Some have suggested that preferences ought to be limited to blacks, a special case of particularly heinous discrimination (although no black was interned during World War II, like Japanese Americans, or shunted off to reservations, like American Indians). But, again, not all blacks have slave ancestors. And not every black was confronted with discrimination or, at least, the same kind of discrimination (among the most obvious variables are geography and occupation).

It is likewise dangerous to generalize among the many different subgroups who make up the group "Hispanic," a social-scientist construct. And many blacks and many Hispanics do not suffer a depressed socioeconomic status, even though they or their ancestors may have suffered discrimination—which makes it impossible to justify a preference for them on the assumption that they do.

It is also a non sequitur to assert that those blacks and Hispanics who did suffer a depressed socioeconomic status and who also may have suffered discrimination became or remained impoverished because of racism. Their individual actions may have had at least as great an impact. Illegitimacy, substance abuse, and poor study and work habits can mire an individual in poverty as surely as racism can. I understand the argument that racism leads to despair and that despair makes bad lifestyle choices more likely, but this is a tenuous sequence, overcome by many. . . .

Finally, it would be desirable if those now penalized by the use of preferences also happened to be the beneficiaries of past discrimination against those now receiving the preferences. There is, however, little if any correlation in this regard. Recent immigrants and children of recent immigrants, descendants of working-class northerners, Midwest farmers' sons, Hasidic Jews, and so on—none of them is likely to have benefited in more than a very indirect way from discrimination against blacks or Hispanics, yet each of them is placed at a competitive disadvantage with them by admission preferences.

The Diversity Argument

The third and final justification for the use of preferences draws heavily from the late Justice Lewis Powell's opinion—joined, incidentally, by no other justice—in *Regents of the University of California v. Bakke:* namely, "the educational benefits that flow from an ethnically diverse student body."

The first problem to note here is that the rationale is "exclusive" as well as "inclusive." If diversity can justify preferences in favor of certain groups that are "underrepresented," then logically it can justify negative weights on those that are "overrepresented." There is simply no way to justify the former without justifying the latter. Saying there are "not enough" blacks and Hispanics is no different from saying that there are "too many" Jews and Asians.

Well, let's press on. What might the "educational benefits" of diversity be? Sometimes it is argued that simply being with people who have a different color or ethnic background is desirable, even if they do not otherwise differ, precisely because this shows students that race and ethnicity do not matter. But this plan will work only if the potentially bigoted student is surrounded by others who really are similar to him in ability. If the minorities admitted into the school are less qualified than the nonminorities, prejudice will be reinforced, not eroded.

Preferences Are Wrong

The oppression of blacks and some other minorities in our country has been grievous, a stain on our history; no honest person will deny that. But the notion that we can redress that historical grievance by giving preference now to persons in the same racial or sexual group as those earlier wronged is a mistake, a blunder. It supposes that rights are possessed by groups, and that therefore advantages given to some minority group now can be payment for earlier injuries to other members of that minority. But moral entitlements are not held by groups. Whites as a group do not have rights, and blacks as a group do not have rights; rights are possessed by persons, individual human persons.

Carl Cohen, *Heritage Lectures*, no. 611, April 29, 1998.

The other possibility is that in fact differences among groups do exist, and that these differences justify preferences to ensure racial and ethnic diversity. Of course, right away it must be acknowledged that not all such differences are important. Maybe some groups, as a whole, have a particular "outlook" or "experience" when it comes to food, but so what? The desired differences ought to relate to the intellectual discipline being taught. Thus, for instance, it is unclear how *any* cultural difference is relevant to graduate work in mathematics.

But there is a more critical point. Given that we might want some particular inner qualities or experiences represented at the university, does it make sense to use race or ethnicity as a proxy for them? Instead, why not select directly for the quality or experience rather than assuming that everyone of a particular race or ethnicity has it and that others do not?

In his opinion, Justice Powell stressed the importance of having students with particular "ideas and mores" and, later, "experiences, outlooks, and ideas," who will "contribute the most to the 'robust exchange of ideas.'" But if we want students with particular ideas, mores, outlooks, and experiences, then why not select those students—rather than assuming that, because a student has a particular color or ancestry, he or she will meet the admission officer's conception of, for instance, a typical black or Hispanic? . . .

Consequences of Discrimination

Still, I am not prepared to say that the claims for benefits from preferences are ludicrous, although obviously I believe each claim is deeply flawed. But the inquiry cannot end with the conclusion that there *might* be something to the claim that the use of preferences has some benefits. We must proceed to ask, Is it likely that those benefits outweigh the costs? And those costs, unlike the claimed benefits, are clear and undeniable.

To begin with, you are discriminating on the basis of race or ethnicity. You are making generalizations about people on the basis of these immutable characteristics. You are then rewarding or punishing them because they happen to have a certain color or ancestors. This practice is unfair to the individual involved—and it is disastrous as social policy. Once discrimination becomes institutionalized, it is very hard to get rid of. You also set a very bad precedent when you give up the principle of nondiscrimination. It is an especially dangerous activity for a state-run institution.

Next, you create resentment among many of those who lose out because of your discrimination. And this resentment is unlikely to be limited in time or scope to the one instance in which it occurs. It is also unlikely to be limited to the immediate victims: their parents, friends, and families will be resentful, too.

You will stigmatize the so-called beneficiaries of the preferences—both in the eyes of others and in their own eyes. You will diminish the accomplishments of those blacks and Hispanics who did not need special treatment. Where preferences are used, people—classmates, future employers—

will assume that a person in the preferred group who was admitted was less qualified than other people who were admitted. And, of course, that is a fair assumption. The whole purpose of the preferences is, after all, to admit those who would otherwise have been rejected as less qualified. It assumes some groups cannot succeed if held to the same standards as others.

You will compromise the mission of the university. You will be making intellectual ability a secondary attribute. You will be tempted to discriminate in your grading, retention, and graduation policies. The school's graduates will be less competent, with all the attendant social and economic costs of that.

Finally, you will be breaking the law. The court of appeals in *Hopwood v. Texas* has ruled, correctly, that the Fourteenth Amendment (which applies to all state schools) and Title VI of the Civil Rights Act of 1964 (which applies to all schools, private and state, that receive federal money) forbid the use of admissions preferences. And the Supreme Court has ruled that section 1981 of title 42 of the U.S. Code bars racial discrimination even by private schools that do not receive federal money. . . .

Which Way Does the Scale Tip?

So, tally up the costs and benefits. *Maybe* there is something to the diversity rationale in some cases, and *maybe* there is something to the remedial and prophylactic rationales in some cases, too, although we have seen that all three rationales are riddled with holes. You still are obliged to consider what is on the other side of the scale: the fact that you are discriminating, the resentment, the stigmatization, the compromising of the mission of the university, and the illegality. Which way does the scale tip? To anyone who is intellectually honest, it is not a close question. Preferences should not be used.

*"Studies with large national samples [prove]
. . . the superiority of bilingual education
programs."*

Schools Should Employ Bilingual Education

Jeff MacSwan

Hispanic students learning English benefit from bilingual education, argues Jeff MacSwan in the following viewpoint. Intensive "English-immersion" programs, which some have lauded as a replacement for bilingual education, result in lower graduation rates for Latino youths, MacSwan points out. It takes years for children whose native language is not English to learn the language well enough to handle subjects that are taught in English—a concern that is taken seriously by bilingual education programs. MacSwan is an assistant professor of curriculum and instruction at Arizona State University.

As you read, consider the following questions:

1. During Tucson's "English Immersion Era," what percentage of Hispanic youths graduated from high school each year?
2. According to MacSwan, bilingual education has helped to boost Tucson's Latino graduation rate to what percentage?
3. How many years does it take the majority of English-language learners to become proficient in the language, according to the author?

Reprinted, with permission, from "Punished for Speaking Spanish? 'Immersion' Drowns the Hopes of Many Hispanic Children," by Jeff MacSwan, *Arizona Republic*, February 28, 1999.

E ver learn a language in 180 days? Ron Unz, a software developer from California, recently visited Arizona to declare that you can. In fact, under his proposed "English for the Children" initiative, if you're a child whose native language is not English, then you must.

The proposed initiative provides that English learners be placed in "structured immersion" (or intensive English as a second language [ESL]) for a period of one year, or 180 school days.

After that, children must be "mainstreamed," or placed in classes in the regular program alongside native English speakers. The initiative would also outlaw *bilingual* education.

The Problem with Immersion Programs

Ironically, Tucson was home to "structured immersion" from 1919 to 1967. As Tucson discovered, the problem with such programs is that they fail to take into account a very important fact: School is primarily about learning content, such as language arts, math and science.

Because they do not understand the language of instruction, children tend to fall behind academically. Despite their ability to engage in simple conversations early on, it takes a number of years to learn English well enough to understand all-English instruction.

During Tucson's English Immersion Era, less than 40 percent of Hispanic children graduated from high school each year.

The enrollment of Hispanic children plummeted to about 25 percent by 1967, at which time the city's school district introduced bilingual education. Today, partly as a result of this innovation, nearly 90 percent of Tucson's Hispanic students graduate.

The Need for Bilingual Education

The Arizona Department of Education reports that students in bilingual programs do better statewide. Studies with large national samples have reached similar conclusions regarding the superiority of bilingual education programs.

Meanwhile, opponents of bilingual education report that only 4 percent of English language learners are reclassified as "English proficient" each year. What they don't tell us is that a full 73 percent of these children are now in Unz-style immersion classes, not bilingual education programs.

Little time has passed since Unz's initiative passed in California, but in Orange Unified School District, where Unz's program was implemented a year early, only six children in 3,549 could be mainstreamed in 1998. That's a failure rate of 99.83 percent for English the Unz Way.

But Unz's group of English-only zealots are not the only folks in Arizona who want to place arbitrary limits on children in bilingual and ESL programs. State Rep. Laura Knaperek recently introduced a bill which passed in the House of Representatives.

This bill limits support for English language learners to only three years. State Superintendent of Public Instruction Lisa Keegan has advocated a limit of four years. These proposals may seem like wise, political compromise to politicians, but the least powerful of Knaperek's and Keegan's constituents—the children who need time to learn English—will view it as heartless and arbitrary.

Why Schools Need Bilingual Education

Now, more and more immigrants are from Latin American countries with poorer educational traditions. Many of these students arrive with limited schooling and limited literacy in their native language and confront educational demands not present decades ago. They do not have sufficient first-language skills or the content knowledge necessary to develop a second language quickly and to comprehend instruction. First and foremost, they must become readers and writers; how can they do so if not taught in a language they already understand?

Ofelia Garcia, *Newsday*, June 4, 1998.

After four years, only 75 percent of English language learners know enough English to participate effectively in mainstream classes, according to Keegan's own report. Knaperek's and Keegan's willingness to close the door on the weakest of the weak speaks to their true commitments as public servants.

Time limits of any sort reflect a basic distrust of learners.

They appear to be guided by an underlying assumption that, if we threaten students enough with failure or expulsion, they will learn English faster, as though they are defiantly resisting the language of economic opportunity which brought them and their families to our state.

Bilingual education programs could be even better for our children. Sen. Joe Eddie Lopez has drafted an important reform bill which will strengthen well-designed bilingual education programs and revamp those in need of help.

It also strengthens parental choice, allowing families to choose the programs they want. Please urge your state senator to oppose the Knaperek bill and to support Lopez's legislation as approved by the Appropriations Committee. [As of February 2000, this legislation has not passed.]

> *"[In] Arizona, which has one of the most disastrous bilingual education systems . . . a pitiful 7 percent of the students [are] able to acquire English proficiency each year."*

Schools Should Not Employ Bilingual Education

Georgie Anne Geyer

In the following viewpoint, syndicated columnist Georgie Anne Geyer contends that Spanish-speaking students benefit more from English-only teaching than they do from bilingual education. English-immersion programs in California, for example, have greatly boosted the standardized test scores of English-language learners, she points out. Bilingual education programs, on the other hand, should be dropped because they result in a very low rate of English proficiency for immigrant students.

As you read, consider the following questions:
1. What is Proposition 227, according to the author?
2. By what percentage did standardized test scores go up after the introduction of English-immersion programs in Oceanside, California, according to Geyer?
3. In Geyer's opinion, what challenges remain for supporters of English-immersion programs?

From "English Only: Success of Immersion Programs Reveals Fallacy of Bilingual Education," by Georgie Anne Geyer, syndicated column of August 25, 1999. Copyright ©1999 Universal Press Syndicate. All rights reserved. Reprinted with permission.

They said it couldn't work. The entire education establishment was convinced that, without the convoluted programs of "bilingual education" it had invested so much in, Spanish-speaking children never would learn anything at all.

Well, not only is it working in California after a remarkably orderly start in 1998, but the new program of "structured English immersion" is working wonders. "English-Only Teaching Is a Surprise Hit," the *Los Angeles Times* was trumpeting as early as January 1999, as it meticulously followed the changes. "Bilingual Classes Ban Gets A in California" was the headline in a major *Washington Times* article in the summer of 1999.

Most important, there now is undeniable proof that the English immersion classes—and that means teaching overwhelmingly in English from the very beginning instead of teaching 90 percent in Spanish and expecting the kids somehow to edge into English—have had stunning results. California's Standardized Testing and Reporting scores, published in the summer of 1999, show that the scores of English learners rose 18 percent in reading, 21 percent in mathematics, 15 percent in language, 21 percent in spelling and 19 percent overall from 1998 to 1999.

Impressive Results from English Immersion

Where English has been thoroughly implemented, and not grudgingly so, the results are even more impressive. In Oceanside, a pretty seaside community between Los Angeles and San Diego, Superintendent Kenneth Noonan had been a staunch supporter of bilingual education for a long time. In fact, he was the founding president of the California Association of Bilingual Educators. But when he was faced with Proposition 227, the citizen initiative that rejected bilingual education by a 61 percent margin in June 1998, Mr. Noonan, himself of Mexican descent, determined to do the best possible job with the new program of structured English immersion.

Consequently, with a school population in which a fifth of the students were of "limited English proficiency," scores in the Oceanside Unified School District went up a whopping

47 percent from 1998 to 1999. In a few districts, some of the score improvements have been as much as 93 percent. And this in a California school system where, under the old bilingual program, only 6.7 percent of the 1.4 million California students with limited English proficiency were graduating to full proficiency every year.

What's more, using a little-known part of Proposition 227, which provides for $50 million to help immigrant parents to learn English, parents are pouring into the special English language classes, thus preparing them to help their children with their schoolwork for the first time.

Reprinted by permission of Mark Thornhill.

Such successes are being reported across the country. Indeed, the *Washington Post* ran a comprehensive article on how well immigrant children are doing under English immersion. Only a few years after their arrival in the United States, many are at the top of their classes. "They've Arrived," the headline read. "Forced to Learn in English, Many Immigrants Excel in School."

Meanwhile, in states such as Arizona, which has one of the most disastrous bilingual education systems in the country, with a pitiful 7 percent of the students able to acquire English proficiency each year, a big fight over changing it has begun. As it now is, critics are calling it "bi-illiteracy." The chairman of the state Senate's education committee calls the whole pathetic process "mass production criminality."

Challenges Remain

Don't get too excited, lest you think the progress in California and elsewhere means the problem has been solved or at least is being seriously addressed across the country. We need to realize that we are dealing with the education establishment's most ideological minds. They will tell you with faith and confidence that the sun comes up in the West. Approach at your own risk then.

At every turn, the bilingual establishment is trying to sabotage the changes wrought by Proposition 227, or "English for the Children," as it is called. Indeed, in a 1999 speech, Eugene Garcia, former director of the federal Education Department's bilingual education office, stated openly that educators were doing everything possible to circumvent Proposition 227. They were feigning compliance.

It is ideologues like those who expect us to believe that one learns English by speaking Spanish who have been in control. But at least in California and elsewhere, that seems to be changing.

Periodical Bibliography

The following articles have been selected to supplement the diverse views presented in this chapter. Addresses are provided for periodicals not indexed in the *Readers' Guide to Periodical Literature*, the *Alternative Press Index*, the *Social Sciences Index*, or the *Index to Legal Periodicals and Books*.

Charles T. Canady and
Robert C. Scott
"Q: Should Washington End All Preferences in Hiring and Contracting?" *Insight*, April 27, 1998. Available from 3600 New York Ave. NE, Washington, DC 20002.

Trevor W. Coleman
"Affirmative Action Wars," *Emerge*, March 1998. Available from One BET Plaza, 1900 W Place NE, Washington, DC 20028-1211.

Charles Fried
"Uneasy Preferences: Affirmative Action, in Retrospect," *American Prospect*, September/October 1999.

Luisa Garro
"Bilingual Schooling That Works," *New York Times*, July 10, 1999.

Glenn Garvin
"Loco, Completamente Loco," *Reason*, January 1998.

Martin Michaelson
"Affirmative Action in College and University Admissions: Yes," *National Forum*, Winter 1999. Available from the Honor Society of Phi Kappa Phi, Box 16000, Louisiana State University, Baton Rouge, LA 70893.

Rosalie Pedalino Porter
"The Case Against Bilingual Education," *Atlantic Monthly*, May 1998.

Eugene Rivers, interviewed by Aaron Gallegos
"A Nation Within a Nation," *Sojourners*, March/April 1998.

Lourdes Rovira
"Let's Not Say Adios to Bilingual Education," *U.S. Catholic*, November 1998.

Stephen Steinberg
"Up from Slavery: The Myth of Black Progress," *New Politics*, Summer 1998.

Ron Unz
"California and the End of White America," *Commentary*, November 1999.

David Wagner
"Race-Based Programs Are on the Defensive," *World & I*, September 1998. Available from 3600 New York Ave. NE, Washington, DC 20002.

CHAPTER 4

How Can Race Relations Be Improved?

Chapter Preface

In 1997, President Bill Clinton announced the beginning of a yearlong "Initiative on Race." Arguing that the public needed to face "the implications of Americans of so many races living and working together as we approach a new century," he established an advisory panel to facilitate a national dialogue on race.

The idea of encouraging communication between whites and minorities as a way to dismantle racism is not new. Since the 1980s, many businesses, universities, social organizations, and religious groups have undertaken cross-racial dialogues to help whites and minorities better understand why they often hold such contrasting views on race relations. During such discussions, whites and minorities are given a chance to see each other as individuals with a variety of backgrounds and opinions—an experience which can help to undercut stereotypes and prejudices, proponents contend. Well-planned and skillfully facilitated community dialogues, argues diversity counselor Andrea Ayvazian, can help Americans "move beyond polite and empty words, beyond slogans and accusations, and beyond the fears and hurts that close us off from one another."

Many critics, however, maintain that most community dialogues on race amount to nothing more than group-therapy-like "whine" sessions. Such allegedly "healing" discussions, they claim, simply encourage exaggerated complaints from people of color who are allowed to bash whites for harboring unconscious racist feelings. In the opinion of columnist Charles Krauthammer, the idea of a national conversation on race is "nonsense": "America's problem is not inhibition. It is exhibition. What the President . . . should be preaching is racial decency. Respect. Restraint. Manners." On the other hand, Baptist pastor Jeff Smith argues that "town meetings . . . are woefully inadequate to confront the deeply rooted issues that continue to keep America a divided nation." Only sustained dialogues—small-group discussions taking place over a period of months or years—can foster genuine racial reconciliation, maintains Smith.

The authors in the following chapter present additional viewpoints on ways to improve race relations.

"[Our] differences do not signal disunity but instead reflect an enhanced strength."

Embracing Racial Diversity Can Help to Unify America

Advisory Board to the President's Initiative on Race

In 1997, President Bill Clinton launched a national initiative on race that was supervised by a multiracial advisory panel. This panel researched racial issues, facilitated a national dialogue on race, and proposed solutions to racial problems. The following viewpoint is excerpted from the advisory board's report to the president, in which the values of cultural and racial diversity are lauded. The board offers several suggestions for improving race relations, such as the recommendation to teach a history that includes minority perspectives and ideas on what individuals can do to help overcome racial prejudice and discrimination.

As you read, consider the following questions:
1. According to the advisory board, what presents a significant barrier to improving race relations?
2. In the opinion of Judith Winston, the director of the race initiative, what do Americans need to recognize about themselves in order to overcome racial divisions?
3. What should an individual do when he or she hears racist or prejudicial comments, according to the authors?

Excerpted from *One America in the Twenty-First Century: Forging a New Future*, a government report from the Advisory Board to the President's Initiative on Race, September 1998.

The recommendations in this Report to the President are intended to preserve the integrity of the principles that lie at the core of our democracy: justice, equality, dignity, respect, and inclusion. It is with these principles in mind that the Advisory Board acted on behalf of the President in this year-long effort. At times, we were met with doubt, distrust, and even disbelief. The negative reactions often seemed to draw more attention than the positive responses to our work. However, in most instances, our efforts were met with both enthusiasm and appreciation for the leadership and the willingness of the President to undertake this unprecedented initiative.

Literally tens of thousands of Americans shared in dialogues to weave our different, and common, experiences together so that paths toward deeper understanding might emerge. While many of the conversations allowed for greater insight and a shared sense of commitment to find ways to advance race relations, some conversations ended without resolution. But that is the nature of dialogue—a process that invites differing points of view and is open to possibilities yet unrecognized. Regardless of the outcome, we learned that there exists a genuine recognition by many people that the challenges presented by racial and ethnic divides in the country must be met. . . .

Building a New Consensus

One of the barriers to improving race relations is our lack of knowledge about our collective past. As Board Chairman John Hope Franklin told us at our first meeting, "The beginning of wisdom is knowledge, and without knowledge of the past we cannot wisely chart our course for the future." A common base of knowledge is essential to genuine racial healing. We do not presume to tell teachers how to teach history, but we believe it is vital to our future that the history we teach accurately reflects our history from the perspective of all Americans, not just the majority population.

Teaching a more inclusive and comprehensive history is just one of the ways we may begin to become more comfortable about our Nation's growing diversity. Today, too many people fear the demographic changes that are occurring and too few people understand the strength that our diversity has always provided. On the other hand, minority communities continue to grapple with issues of inclusion or exclusion, which are often expressed in terms of identity politics that seem to reject the notion of common values and ideals. During this delicate period of redefining the American policy, we must exercise extra caution so that we may better understand and value our differences and understand that those differences do not signal disunity but instead reflect an enhanced strength.

Reaching Beyond the Choir

We were quite successful, we believe, in energizing people who are already involved in activities designed to bridge racial divisions—the so-called choir. We do not minimize this accomplishment because we believe that even the choir needs reinforcement, recognition, and inspiration to sustain its efforts. At the same time, even stronger efforts must be made to reach beyond the choir to the vast majority of Americans who are people of goodwill, but who fail to recognize the importance to their lives and the lives of their children of overcoming racial divisions and narrowing racial disparities. If America is to achieve her full potential and if our children are to have an opportunity to achieve the same standard of living we have achieved, we must, as Executive Director of the Race Initiative Judith Winston warned:

> Acknowledge the fact that most Americans are not, and do not consider themselves racist, but they have responses to people who are different than they on the basis of race that suggest that they have internalized—we have internalized—these racist concepts and stereotypes. . . . We have to find a way of engaging people, helping people to become engaged in conversations that are not confrontational and that are constructive.

During 1997 and 1998, we have planted seeds of racial healing, seeds that can erase "the fault line of race." We have traveled to communities in every region of the country to discuss issues of race. While these issues are often laden with emotion, we have tried to move the discussion beyond the polarizing impact of debate to the unifying impact of reasoned dialogue.

For it is reasoned dialogue, and not divisive debate, that ultimately will ease the fault line caused by race and strengthen our resolve to work together to build an American community worthy of the principles and values we espouse.

Ten Things Every American Should Do

One of the most striking findings from our work is that many Americans are willing to accept that racial prejudice, privilege, and disparities are major problems confronting our Nation. Many of them told us that they would welcome concrete advice about what they should do. To fill that need, we offer a brief list of actions that individual Americans could take that would increase the momentum that will make us one America in the 21st century.

1. *Make a commitment to become informed about people from other races and cultures.* Read a book, see a movie, watch a play, or attend a cultural event that will inform you and your family about the history and current lives of a group different than your own.

2. *If it is not your inclination to think about race, commit at least 1 day each month to thinking about how issues of racial prejudice and privilege might be affecting each person you come in contact with that day.* The more that people think about how issues of race affect each person, the easier it will be for Americans to talk honestly about race and eliminate racial divisions and disparities.

3. *In your life, make a conscious effort to get to know people of other races.* Also, if your religious community is more racially isolated than your local area, encourage it to form faith partnerships with racially different faith groups.

4. *Make a point to raise your concerns about comments or actions that appear prejudicial, even if you are not the targets of these actions.* When people say or do things that are clearly racially biased, speak out against them, even if you are not the target. When people do things that you think *might be* influenced by prejudice, raise your concerns that the person or institution seriously consider the role that racial bias might play, even unconsciously.

5. *Initiate a constructive dialogue on race within your workplace, school, neighborhood, or religious community.* The *One*

America Dialogue Guide provides some useful ideas about how to construct a dialogue and lists some organizations that conduct dialogues and can help with facilitation.

6. *Support institutions that promote racial inclusion.* Watch television programs and movies that offer racially diverse casts that reflect the real world instead of those perpetuating an inaccurately segregated view of America. Support companies and non-profit organizations that demonstrate a commitment to racial inclusion in personnel and subcontracting. Write the institutions to let them know of your support for what they are doing.

7. *Participate in a community project to reduce racial disparities in opportunity and well-being.* These projects can also be good ways of getting to know people from other backgrounds.

Cultural Citizenship

Multicultural theorists assume that we cannot unite the nation around its democratic ideals by forcing people from different racial, ethnic and cultural groups to leave their cultures and languages at the schoolhouse door. An important principle of a democratic society is that citizens will voluntarily participate in the commonwealth and that their participation will enrich the nation-state.

When citizens participate in society and bring their cultural strengths to the national civic culture, both they and the nation are enriched. Renato Rosaldo, the Stanford anthropologist, calls this kind of civic participation *cultural citizenship.*

We can create an inclusive, democratic and civic national community only when we change the center to make it more inclusive and reflective of the diversity that enriches our nation.

James A. Banks, *School Administrator*, May 1999.

8. *Insist that institutions that teach us about our community accurately reflect the diversity of our Nation.* Encourage our schools to provide festivals and celebrations that authentically celebrate the history, literature, and cultural contributions of the diverse groups that make up the United States. Insist that our children's schools' textbooks, curricula, and libraries provide a full understanding of the contributions of different racial groups and an accurate description of our historic and ongoing struggle for racial inclusion. Insist that

our news sources—whether print, television, or radio—include racially diverse opinions, story ideas, analyses, and experts. Support ethnic studies programs in our colleges and universities so people are educated and critical dialogue about race is stimulated.

9. *Visit other areas of the city, region, or country that allow you to experience parts of other cultures, beyond their food.* If you have an attitude that all people have histories, cultures, and contributions about which you could benefit from learning, it is usually not difficult to find someone who enjoys exposing others to their culture.

10. *Encourage groups you can influence (whether you work as a volunteer or employee) to examine how they can increase their commitment to reducing racial disparities, lessening discrimination, and improving race relations.* Whether you are a member of a small community group or executive of a large corporation, virtually everyone can attempt to influence a group to join the national effort to build one America.

"Ethnic diversity' is merely racism in a politically correct disguise."

Embracing Racial Diversity Is Counterproductive

Michael S. Berliner and Gary Hull

In the following viewpoint, Michael S. Berliner and Gary Hull contend that emphasizing racial diversity—particularly in educational settings—is harmful. Although the "diversity movement" alleges that it is seeking to eliminate racism and promote tolerance, it actually increases racism by fostering the belief that one's character and identity are determined by skin color. Such highlighting of race leads to segregation and racial divisiveness, the authors maintain. Berliner is executive director of the Ayn Rand Institute in Marina del Rey, California. Hull is a senior writer for the Ayn Rand Institute.

As you read, consider the following questions:

1. In what way does the destruction of an individual's confidence in himself foster racism, according to Berliner and Hull?
2. What kind of diversity is forbidden on college campuses, in the authors' opinion?
3. In the authors' view, what theory of human nature should universities promote?

Reprinted, with permission, from "Diversity and Multiculturalism: The New Racism," by Michael S. Berliner and Gary Hull, a 1998 article on the website of the Ayn Rand Institute at http://multiculturalism.aynrand.org/diversity.html.

I s ethnic diversity an "absolute essential" of a college education? UCLA's Chancellor Charles Young thinks so. Ethnic diversity is clearly the purpose of affirmative action, which Young is defending against a long-overdue assault. But far from being essential to a college education, such diversity is a sure road to its destruction. "Ethnic diversity" is merely racism in a politically correct disguise.

Many people have a very superficial view of racism. They see it as merely the belief that one race is superior to another. It is much more than that. It is a fundamental (and fundamentally wrong) view of human nature. Racism is the notion that one's race determines one's identity. It is the belief that one's convictions, values and character are determined not by the judgment of one's mind but by one's anatomy or "blood."

This view causes people to be condemned (or praised) based on their racial membership. In turn, it leads them to condemn or praise others on the same basis. In fact, one can gain an authentic sense of pride only from one's own achievements, not from inherited characteristics.

The Spread of Racism

The spread of racism requires the destruction of an individual's confidence in his own mind. Such an individual then anxiously seeks a sense of identity by clinging to some group, abandoning his autonomy and his rights, allowing his ethnic group to tell him what to believe. Because he thinks of himself as a racial entity, he feels "himself" only among others of the same race. He becomes a separatist, choosing his friends—and enemies—based on ethnicity. This separatism has resulted in the spectacle of student-segregated dormitories and segregated graduations.

The diversity movement claims that its goal is to extinguish racism and build tolerance of differences. This is a complete sham. One cannot teach students that their identity is determined by skin color and expect them to become colorblind. One cannot espouse multiculturalism and expect students to see each other as individual human beings. One cannot preach the need for self-esteem while destroying the faculty which makes it possible: reason. One cannot teach collective identity and expect students to have self-esteem. Advocates of "diversity" are true racists in the basic meaning of that term: they see the world through colored lenses, colored by race and gender. To the multiculturalist, race is what counts—for values, for thinking, for human identity in general. No wonder racism is increasing: colorblindness is now considered evil, if not impossible. No wonder people don't treat each other as individuals: to the multiculturalist, they aren't.

Institutionalized Separatism

Advocates of "diversity" claim it will teach students to tolerate and celebrate their differences. But the "differences" they have in mind are racial differences, which means we're being urged to glorify race, which means we're being asked to institutionalize separatism. "Racial identity" erects an unbridgeable gulf between people, as though they were different species, with nothing fundamental in common. If that were true—if "racial identity" determined one's values and thinking methods—there would be no possibility for understanding or cooperation among people of different races.

Why Diversity Is Divisive

It is now taken as a virtual axiom that the way to cure racism is through the promulgation of racial and ethnic diversity within corporations, universities, government agencies and other institutions. The diversity movement has many facets: diversity awareness, diversity training, diversity hiring and admissions, diversity promotions, and diversity accommodations (e.g., black student organizations and facilities at universities). The common feature in all these facets is: racial preference.

If diversity is the cure, however, why, instead of promoting racial harmony, has it brought racial division and conflict? The answer is not hard to discover. The unshakable fact is that you cannot cure racism with racism. To accept the diversity premise means to think in racial terms rather than in terms of individual character or merit.

Edwin A. Locke, Ayn Rand Institute website, 1998.

Advocates of "diversity" claim that because the real world is diverse, the campus should reflect that fact. But why should a campus population "reflect" the general population (particularly the ethnic population)? No answer. In fact, the purpose of a university is to impart knowledge and develop reasoning, not to be a demographic mirror of society.

Racism, not any meaningful sense of diversity, guides today's intellectuals. The educationally significant diversity that exists in "the real world" is intellectual diversity, i.e., the diversity of ideas. But such diversity—far from being sought after—is virtually forbidden on campus. The existence of "political correctness" blasts the academics' pretense at valuing real diversity. What they want is abject conformity.

The only way to eradicate racism on campus is to scrap racist programs and the philosophic ideas that feed racism. Racism will become an ugly memory only when universities teach a valid concept of human nature: one based on the tenets that the individual's mind is competent, that the human intellect is efficacious, that we possess free will, that individuals are to be judged as individuals—and that deriving one's identity from one's race is a corruption—a corruption appropriate to Nazi Germany, not to a nation based on freedom and independence.

"*Memorializing our slave past [is] important for the present.*"

Whites Should Apologize to Blacks for Slavery

Naomi Wolf

Whites as a group should formally apologize to African Americans for the enslavement of their ancestors, argues Naomi Wolf in the following viewpoint. Such an apology, she contends, would not be a declaration of personal guilt but rather a national expression of regret about a historical atrocity. She maintains that an apology for slavery would help to end America's persistent denial about its racial problems and foster racial reconciliation. Wolf is a writer, feminist theorist, and editorial columnist.

As you read, consider the following questions:

1. Where are some places in which America's "willful amnesia" about slavery is evident, according to Wolf?
2. In the author's opinion, what has happened as a result of the dominant culture's denial about slavery?
3. According to Wolf, what happened during a presentation by spiritualist Marianne Williamson in which whites apologized to blacks for racism?

Reprinted, by permission of the author, from "Who's Sorry Now?" by Naomi Wolf, *George*, August 1998.

W e build memorials to what we want to remember, but a glance at our public monuments also shows just what we want to forget. Just off the Mall in Washington, D.C., there's a vast museum devoted to a holocaust that took place in Europe; near the Potomac, there's a beloved memorial to a slaughter that unfolded in Southeast Asia. But you'd have to look long and hard over the American landscape to find any prominent recognition of our own homegrown holocaust—of the 250 years during which up to one American in five was held, scourged, and bred as chattel.

A Willful Amnesia

America has a willful amnesia about its slave past. Daily life in Colonial Williamsburg has been painstakingly re-created for the sake of tourists. In the West, towns re-enact the days of the gold rush. But at the sites of the notorious slave markets—where thousands of African families were dispersed while sustaining the economies that supported white families—there is little or no commemoration. Ellis Island's makeover is a gleaming piece of historical preservation; but in Auburn, New York, the house of Harriet Tubman, which was a famous station on the Underground Railroad, now lies in disrepair, its preservation left to the amateur efforts of local citizens who raise funds to maintain it. The slave quarters at Mount Vernon carefully explain the production of horseshoes and tallow: Tools are displayed, but not whips or shackles. No multimedia archives bother to chronicle the histories of, and relationships between, the enslaved Americans who served the father of our country. Little attention is paid to the bitter irony that while George Washington allowed his slaves to wed, the state of Virginia refused to legally recognize those unions.

White America wants to forget. In the 1970s, the miniseries *Roots* was a major pop culture event because it gave names and faces to historical shadows, but its theme was palatable to whites only because it led, ultimately, to assimilation and redemption. In contrast, Steven Spielberg's recent *Amistad*—a straightforward and unsettling account of the subjection of Africans in the slave trade—sank like a stone.

Plenty of whites would say that memorializing our slave

past is worse than unimportant, that it is destructive to the present. Controversy attended efforts to obtain congressional funding for a museum of slavery on the Mall. Southern struggles over the Confederate flag are routine and bitter. Whites' reactions to blacks' insistence on memorializing slavery are strong: "I didn't own any slaves. Why should I apologize?" as one recent caller to a talk-radio station characteristically argued. When Congressman Tony P. Hall, a white Democrat from Ohio, raised the subject of an apology for slavery as a "step toward healing," he was deluged with criticism. President Bill Clinton typically waffled on this issue when, in August 1997, he chose to leave the decision on whether to apologize for slavery up to his race advisory board. Eight months later, inching toward a more complete gesture, he sort of apologized for the slave trade—in Africa, to the descendants of Africans who were left behind by it; not in America to the descendants of those who were captured and bred in captivity. "The United States has not always done the right thing by Africa," he said with a truly farcical note of understatement. "Going back to the time before we were even a nation, European Americans received the fruits of the slave trade . . . and we were wrong in that."

Why does an apology matter? Why is memorializing our slave past important for the present? These things matter because without them, both sides remain stuck. The mass denial of slavery by the dominant culture creates what denial creates in any dysfunctional family: inflamed articulation of the denied truth by the injured party. The more one family member silences, the more the other symbolically over-emotes. When a black man was recently dragged to his death by three whites in Jasper, Texas, whites quoted in news coverage swore that the savage murder was an isolated event, as if they were unconscious of the history of lynching in towns just like theirs. In reaction to such denial, the African-Americans quoted were inclined toward conspiracy theories. "At this point," one woman reportedly said, "I'll believe anything."

How would proper memorials of slavery heal this stalemate? Memorials reflect the depth of our caring. As a Jew, I know rage wells within me toward contemporary Germans when I see a cheap tin marker over a subway entrance in the heart of Berlin commemorating a roundup of local Jews. The slightness of the marker undermines my trust in my German peers—even though the historic tragedy is now distant from us.

Why Apologies Matter

Apologies between groups matter for the same reason they matter between individuals in intimate relationships: They help keep the relationship healthy. The recent wave of international apologies speaks to the power of this fact. Why should we care whether Switzerland returns what are often insignificant amounts of money to Jews? Not because of the money but because of the lingering denial. Why did the pope's semi-apology for the Catholic Church's collusion with Nazism reinforce Jewish distrust of Catholicism? Precisely because of its tone of self-exoneration. In contrast, France's unstinting apology for its collusion with the Vichy government and Australia's wholehearted Sorry Day, in which the entire continent expresses regret for separating Aboriginal children from their parents, will both go a long way toward genuine healing—the kind we in this country should note with envy.

Finally, particularly where children are concerned, apolo-

Words That Should Not Remain Unspoken

An apology [for slavery] from Congress would send a powerful message. "I am sorry" is the first step of any person trying to right a wrong. These words are the foundation for beginning again, part of the price for restoring lost trust, and necessary to move forward constructively. Yet in the case of our nation's greatest moral failing, speaking those words is a step the US has not taken.

We have pursued countless policies toward the goal of healing. We have been enriched by the determination of African-Americans to overcome the problems rooted in their ancestors' enslavement. But neither their success nor the blood spilled in our Civil War excuses our continuing silence.

The words of an apology may not bring peace. They won't reach any of those directly affected, but they will echo to future generations. They are words that should not remain unspoken.

Tony P. Hall, *Christian Science Monitor*, July 9, 1997.

---

gies reflect the value assigned to a given relationship. Without an apology from whites for the centuries during which black children were bought and sold, black kids grow up wondering if the dominant culture will ever value them enough for their efforts within the system to really work. The fact is, conspiracies against black Americans have been real. Slavery itself was a conspiracy. So were the post-Reconstruction years, when whites banded together to cheat blacks out of fair prices for their cotton and white police forces conspired to frame black defendants. Without an apology that acknowledges this reality, black off-the-wall conspiracy theorizing will continue to assert itself. Hence, for example, the widespread beliefs that the CIA invented AIDS and that the Los Angeles Police Department framed O.J. Simpson.

An apology in this case is not an expression of personal guilt. It is an expression of regret, of shared sorrow. Popular spiritualist Marianne Williamson, who is often mocked for saying things America isn't ready to hear, conducts an experiment with her audiences: She has white people stand and apologize to blacks in the audience for racism and the harm it has inflicted upon their families and children. I watched this once, squirming with discomfort; I was sure it would be offensive, a sham, superficial, insulting, phony—all the things we fear when the issue of an apology comes up. To my astonishment, after the apology the mood in the room changed in a way I have never before felt in America: There was an almost tangible lightening of tension for both the blacks and the whites. It was a mood in which one could actually move on. As one old black woman said, with tears running down her cheeks, "I've been waiting my whole life to hear a white man say that to me."

In a bad marriage, every little friction symbolizes the larger sense of being held in contempt or feeling betrayed. That's where we are now. In a good marriage, a fight, no matter how bad it gets, is just a fight. That's where an apology can take us. So in the interest of starting with what I can, I want to say, for the record, about this great harm: I am so sorry.

"Slavery existed all over this planet. . . .
Why then a national apology for a
worldwide evil? Is a national apology for
murder next?"

An Apology for Slavery Would Not Advance Race Relations

Thomas Sowell

In the following viewpoint, economist and syndicated columnist Thomas Sowell argues against the proposal that whites should apologize to blacks for slavery. Slavery was a worldwide phenomenon that existed among all races; no one group should be singled out as perpetrators, he points out. Moreover, the majority of white Americans who lived during slavery were too poor to own slaves, and many of today's whites are descendants of Europeans who immigrated to America after slavery. Having whites apologize for something that they are not responsible for would only increase racial tensions, Sowell concludes.

As you read, consider the following questions:

1. In what ways does the idea of an apology for slavery reveal a misunderstanding of history, in Sowell's opinion?
2. What ethnic group is the word *slave* derived from, according to the author?
3. In Sowell's view, how might an apology for slavery affect blacks?

Reprinted from "National Apology a Nutty Proposal," Thomas Sowell's syndicated column of July 2, 1997, by permission of Thomas Sowell and Creators Syndicate, Inc.

O ne of the many painful signs of what mindless mush we take seriously today is a proposal in Congress to have a national apology for slavery. This is insanity in so many ways that it is hard to know where to start. [As of February 2000, this proposal has not been ratified.]

First of all, slavery is not something like stepping on someone's toe accidentally, where you can just say "excuse me." If the people who actually enslaved their fellow human beings were alive today, hanging would be too good for them. An apology would be an insult.

If an apology would make no sense coming from those who were personally guilty, what sense does it make for someone else to apologize for them today? An apology for what somebody else did makes sense only if you abandon the whole idea of personal responsibility. Unfortunately, too many people have already done that, with disastrous consequences.

A Gross Ignorance of History

A national apology also betrays a gross ignorance of history. Slavery existed all over this planet, among people of every color, religion and nationality. Why then a national apology for a worldwide evil? Is a national apology for murder next?

By making this a national issue and a racial issue, the whole nature and magnitude of slavery are distorted and grossly understated. If slavery were just a matter of whites enslaving blacks, the number of slaves would have been a small fraction of the actual total around the world. And if it were just a matter of slaves being taken from Africa to the United States, that would be an even smaller fraction.

There are islands in the Caribbean that imported more slaves from Africa than the United States did and Brazil imported 6 times as many. The Islamic countries of the Middle East and North Africa took even more slaves from Africa than the entire Western Hemisphere. Why then is slavery being spoken of as if it were a national problem peculiar to the United States?

As for the racial aspect of slavery, for most of the thousands of years of its existence, slavery had nothing to do with race. It was a question of who was vulnerable and who had the power to take advantage of them. Only after centuries of consolidation of much of Europe and Asia into strong national states were large regions of sub-Saharan Africa left as one of the few remaining sources of huge numbers of vulnerable people.

Reprinted by permission of Jimmy Margulies.

But Europeans had enslaved other Europeans, long before they began enslaving Africans. Meanwhile, those Africans who did have strong states had been enslaving other Africans for centuries before they began selling some of them to Europeans, to take to the Western Hemisphere. So did Asians enslave other Asians, as well as enslaving any Europeans or Africans who were available.

An Atrocious Idea

Are those people who want the United States to apologize for slavery also demanding that Africans, Asians, and Western Hemisphere Indians likewise apologize for the same thing? And surely they are not demanding that black Americans as well as white Americans apologize, even though thousands of blacks owned slaves in antebellum New Orleans alone.

What about the majority of white Americans, whose families were too poor to own any slaves? Are they to apologize too? What about those white Americans whose ancestors were still in Europe during the whole era of slavery? The largest-scale immigration to the United States from Europe occurred after the Civil War.

If this apology is going to be by race, who is going to apologize to all the whites who were enslaved around the world—especially the Slavs, from whom the very word "slave" is derived, in both European languages and in Arabic? White slaves were still being bought and sold in Egypt, years after the Emancipation Proclamation had freed blacks in the United States.

The idea of inherited racial guilt—a Nazi conception—behind the proposed apology would do nothing to heal the racial divisions in this country today. Instead, it would promote further polarization.

What would this apology do for blacks?

Is a heightened sense of grievance an asset or a liability in the job market? In education? In human relations across racial lines? Is looking backward the way to prepare for the future?

If neither blacks nor whites, nor American society, are likely to benefit on net balance from this proposed apology, why is such political grandstanding being taken seriously?

"Through [dialogue], people who hold differing views learn about and come to appreciate the life experiences of others."

Cross-Cultural Dialogue Can Benefit Race Relations

Sanford Cloud Jr.

Sanford Cloud Jr. is president and CEO of the National Conference for Community and Justice, a New York–based organization that works to fight bias and racism in the United States. In the following viewpoint, Cloud argues that cross-cultural dialogues are beneficial because they enable individuals to understand each other across racial and ethnic lines. Well-planned dialogues can profoundly change race relations as people come to recognize bias and discover new ways to address bigotry and discrimination.

As you read, consider the following questions:

1. In what way does Cloud distinguish a cross-cultural dialogue from a onetime conversation on human relations?
2. What do facilitators usually do at the beginning of a cross-cultural dialogue, according to the author?
3. According to Cloud, what was the result of the "Anytown" prejudice-reduction program in Alabama?

Reprinted from "A National Dialogue on Race Can Be More than Mere Talk," by Sanford Cloud Jr., *The Christian Science Monitor*, March 5, 1998, by permission of the author.

When President Bill Clinton called on the nation to conduct a national dialogue on race, he challenged us to engage in conversations about our personal views, biases, and how we relate to people different from ourselves. While some have responded positively, others have disparaged the idea as mere talk, devoid of real action.

These critics fail to see that facilitated dialogues on human relations issues—as opposed to daily chats, one-time conversations, or debates—are action. Well-structured town halls and conversations on intergroup relations are important. They are a taking-off point for cross-cultural dialogue.

But they are not dialogue. True dialogue requires a commitment. Through it, people who hold differing views learn about and come to appreciate the life experiences of others.

The Need for Cross-Cultural Dialogue

America needs dialogue. Most of us live and socialize in isolated communities, notwithstanding statistics indicating that our broader environments are increasingly diverse. It's no surprise that people often view themselves and those who are different through a homogenous lens, perpetuating stereotypes and bias. Structured dialogue can open that lens to reveal our hidden assumptions and suspicions about others. By sitting down and talking this talk, we become able to walk the walk of collaborators and community problem-solvers.

Cross-cultural dialogue is not a new concept, nor is it some obscure scientific endeavor too difficult for the ordinary person. It starts with trained facilitators and people whose group identifications and life experiences differ. The facilitator keeps the exchange focused and helps participants get to the issues.

Most dialogues engage people who are not the same. Sometimes there are differences of faith or color. Sometimes differences of economic strata, gender, sexual orientation, or age. Diverse dialogue is best, however, when we convene people who hold divergent perspectives and opposing political and social ideologies. Only then can we avoid preaching to the choir.

Facilitators start by helping participants identify the challenges of creating a safe environment and choose guidelines to govern their honest interactions. These rules vary depending on the people present, but some regularly appear on the list.

The Benefits of Sustained Dialogue

Participants have learned that one of the opportunities sustained dialogue offers is the time, discipline, restraint, and comfort level with each other necessary to explore relationships in depth before acting. A frequent tendency in race relations is for people to content themselves with engaging in common action without ever probing the essence of race relationships. The dialogue provides the opportunity to do that, and participants frequently confirm the benefits of this process.

Harold H. Saunders, *Connections*, December 1998.

Participants often stress the importance of listening actively—rather than engaging in whispered quips spoken in the ear of the person sitting next to them. Other rules often include honesty—to the extent one is able—and confidentiality. Each set of guidelines is unique but provides the groundwork for the discussions to follow.

From there, the process can vary, depending on the facilitator. Sharing personal experiences can lead to the recognition of bias, to an understanding of how it feels to experience bigoted acts, or to hear racist or sexist statements. Often, participants start with themselves, learning to recognize their unspoken assumptions about others. This can start an exploration of racism and power in America as a whole.

Life-Changing Conversations

Such conversations are powerful. They can lead to a changed way of looking at other people and a new openness to working with them. We know this from the young people who attended our residential "Anytown" program in prejudice reduction in Alabama, and subsequently reunited to help rebuild a burned church. And from an African-American professional living in a mostly white community who decided not to move after participating in local dialogues. Instead, she became a community leader and chairwoman of an effort called "Honest Conversations."

The power of dialogue is evident in its continuing impact. In Cincinnati, we conduct "living room dialogues" with government officials, corporate executives, and academics, among others. Often, they take what they've learned with them: One executive returned to his business and implemented dialogue opportunities for employees.

In the end, the success of dialogue is difficult to measure. Statistics don't tell us about improved life experiences, the extent to which prejudiced responses are curbed and human relations enriched. Nor do we have reliable measures for the problems that do not arise because there is a person present who has learned through dialogue how to confront prejudice constructively and create alternative solutions. Yet these results are tangible to those who experience them.

It's time to accept the challenge of improving our intergroup relations by committing, person by person, community by community, to engaging in a human relations dialogue. If we do, we will create change. This is serious work. If we do it well, we will lay the foundation on which to build an America that embraces all of us, not just some of us.

*"The whole conception of a presidentially
mandated national conversation is
nonsense, indeed pernicious nonsense."*

The Benefits of Cross-Cultural Dialogue Are Exaggerated

Charles Krauthammer

In the following viewpoint, editorial columnist Charles Krauthammer decries the notion that Americans would benefit from more cross-cultural dialogue. Discussing people's innermost feelings about race is not likely to bring about racial healing—and could even be harmful, Krauthammer maintains. He contends that racial prejudice is best countered by courtesy, education, and the enforcement of civil rights laws.

As you read, consider the following questions:
1. According to Krauthammer, what recent events reveal that America is obsessed with race?
2. What do civil rights laws mandate, in the author's opinion?
3. What process assists the decline of racism over a period of several generations, in Krauthammer's view?

Reprinted from "Not Enough Conversation?" by Charles Krauthammer, *Time*,
December 22, 1997, by permission of *Time* magazine. Copyright ©1997 Time Inc.

S cientific ideas don't die, they just fade away into popular culture. Psychoanalysis is as dead a science as alchemy. But its central idea, that somehow catharsis leads to cure, lives on—rages on—in Oprah and Geraldo and Ricki Lake and the whole steaming psychic stew that is our confessional culture.

No serious scientist would credit the notion, both unverified and unverifiable, that recalling the repressed, articulating the instinctual, magically undoes the inhibitions and pathologies of life. But no matter. So thoroughly has this fable soaked into the culture that it is now mere conventional wisdom that if we just let it all out from the deep recesses of our souls—the anger, the fear, the prejudice, whatever—we will all be better off.

Not surprisingly, therefore, President Clinton, whose political genius lies in his capacity for expressing, indeed embodying, the zeitgeist of the moment, has seized upon catharsis as his special contribution to dealing with America's racial agonies. Rather than undertaking, say, some vast, expensive and real program to improve inner-city schools, he has called for a "national conversation on race."

Because talk is cheap? Perish the thought. Because in confronting our deepest racial feelings—even if emotions are "rubbed raw," he averred—we will emerge better and stronger.

And so for the two hours of his recent town meeting in Akron, Ohio, the President searched and scratched, picked and poked to bring repressed truth and bias and hurt to the surface. Such was his attempt to start a "national conversation on race." It managed to go nowhere.

It had to. The whole conception of a presidentially mandated national conversation is nonsense, indeed pernicious nonsense. It is nonsense, first, to think that America suffers from a dearth of conversation about race. We are obsessed with race. We can't stop talking about race. Prop. 209, O.J., Piscataway, the gerrymandering cases, race and the death penalty, race and the law schools, race and the Oscars, race and baseball (black attendance is down): Is there an issue under the American sun that has not been given a racial cast?

An angry, hectored basketballer assaults his coach, and within days Johnnie Cochran turns up at the player's side and the airwaves are filled with agonized exegeses of the black player–white coach issue. Why, the Shakespeare Theatre in Washington is playing Othello in reverse colors: a white man (Patrick Stewart) is Othello; Iago, Desdemona and everyone else is black. Not enough conversation?

And, second, it is pernicious nonsense to think that bringing out the deepest, rawest, most unspoken parts of our souls is somehow the road to racial healing. Anyone who has actually done real psychotherapy, in which people really pour out their souls (in my 20s, I practiced psychiatry), knows how dangerous, delicate and often destructive such an exercise can be—even in the privacy, confidentiality and highly ritualized setting of the doctor-patient relationship. But large groups? Of strangers? On live national TV? Led by a well-meaning but astute and cunning pol?

Race Relations Therapy?

A therapeutic model of group dynamics seems to underlie the president's initiative [on race]. We are supposed to be getting our long-hidden fears, resentments and frustrations out in the open. "Be blunt," Clinton instructed his Akron audience [in 1997]. Yet, absent a relationship of trust having been established among the parties to the conversation and without the privacy that ensures one's unguarded comments will not be taken out of context, this is a vain aspiration. A nation cannot talk like a family, no matter how earnest and articulate its political leaders might be.

Glenn Loury, *Washington Post National Weekly Edition*, December 15, 1997.

America is a society already so dedicated to free expression and emotional openness as to astonish the rest of a more reticent world. The last thing this steaming multiracial, multi-ethnic, multi-everything cauldron of 260 million souls requires is yet more rawness in our national life.

America's problem is not inhibition. It is exhibition. What the President and the polity and the pedagogues should be preaching is racial decency. Respect. Restraint. Manners. The lesson ought to be: Whatever your innermost feelings—and we have no idea, despite the claims of pop psychology, how to change inner feelings—we demand certain behavior. That is what the civil rights laws are about. They

175

do not mandate a pure society. They mandate right conduct amid impurity.

The decline of racial prejudice comes over generations, as children are taught, as today's children are indeed taught, the fundamental moral equality of all peoples and the fundamental silliness—apart from the immorality—of distinctions based on race. (And we certainly don't help teach our children indifference to race when we perpetuate social and political policies, such as preferential treatment based on race, that insist on the centrality of race consciousness.)

Akron was more than just another example of this President's belief in the therapeutic effects of talk, of his conviction that the major role of government is not to do but to discuss. It embodied perfectly the vacuousness of the race policy of an Administration that has U-turned twice on the landmark Piscataway case—first joining, then opposing, then supporting again the suit of a white teacher fired to make room for a black colleague.

A President flummoxed by the dilemmas of race chooses to talk them into extinction. No dice. Talk is not a cure. It is a dodge.

"Inter-ethnic anti-racism is emerging as a tactical necessity."

Interethnic Alliances Should Be Formed

George Lipsitz

Disempowered minorities should form alliances across racial and ethnic lines, argues George Lipsitz in the following viewpoint. When people of color try to overcome oppression, the gains that they make too often occur at the expense of other minorities. He points out that those in power typically prefer to have minorities fighting each other because interethnic disunity helps elites maintain their dominance. Racial minorities and other oppressed people must join forces if they wish to create a more just society, the author concludes. Lipsitz is a professor of ethnic studies at the University of California in San Diego. He is also the author of *The Possessive Investment in Whiteness: How White People Profit from Identity Politics.*

As you read, consider the following questions:

1. According to Lipsitz, in what ways do those in power lead various minority groups to work against one another?
2. What are some of the advantages of cross-racial alliances, in the author's opinion?
3. In Lipsitz's view, how does the work of the Asian Immigrant Women Advocates illustrate the need for coalitions across race, class, and gender lines?

Reprinted from "Like Crabs in a Barrel: Why Interethnic Antiracism Matters Now," by George Lipsitz, *Colorlines*, Winter 1999, by permission of *Colorlines*, www.colorlines.com.

In places near the ocean where merchants sell live crabs, they display their wares in open barrels. When the crabs try to escape by climbing up the sides of the barrel, they always fail. As soon as one starts to climb, it gets pulled back down by the others, who are also trying to escape.

When we try to overcome racism, sexism, homophobia, or class oppression, we often find ourselves in the position of crabs in a barrel. We work as hard as we can, but all our efforts fail to free us. Instead of pulling ourselves up, we only pull someone else down.

It is not hard to figure out why this happens. People with power want us to be divided and to fight each other so we will not unite and fight them. If any of us make gains, they want us to make them at each other's expense instead of demanding a fundamental redistribution of resources and power.

A New Model Every Year

This "divide and conquer" strategy has been used more and more in recent years. Malcolm X used to say that racism was like a Cadillac because they came out with a new model every year. There is always racism, but it is not always the same racism. Unlike past segregation and white supremacy which produced a relatively uniform system of exclusion, today's racism employs practices that produce differentiation rather than uniformity, that give excluded groups decisively different relationships to the same oppression.

For example, the opponents of affirmative action make appeals to Asian Americans, arguing that its dismantling will secure "advantages" for Asians that now go to blacks and Latinos. Anti-immigrant groups try to enlist African Americans in efforts to deprive Asian American and Latino immigrants of social services, health care, and education on the grounds that immigrants are responsible for the declines in economic status and political power experienced by blacks in recent years. Racist legislators intent upon dismantling the political gains won by African Americans over the past three decades invite Latinos to support budget cuts, redistricting, term limits, and other measures designed to undercut the seniority, control over resources, and political influence of black legislators.

At the same time, enemies of rights for women and gays and lesbians seek alliances with men of color. They encourage men from aggrieved racial groups to make gains within their own groups rather than outside them, to gain power at the expense of women and gays and lesbians in their own communities rather than at the expense of wealthy white men with power.

These new divisions can also produce unexpected affiliations and alliances. Attacks on bilingual education and immigrants' rights harm both Latinos and Asian Americans. Irrational and alarmist policies about AIDS stigmatize both homosexuals and Haitians. Puerto Ricans on the mainland are both Spanish speakers from a colonized homeland, like Mexicans, and U.S. citizens, like blacks. Filipinos are noncitizen immigrants from Asia, but they share with Mexicans the experience of being immigrants from a Catholic nation colonized by Spain whose patron saint is the Virgin of Guadalupe.

Inter-Ethnic Anti-Racism

Yet the same forces that create unexpected affinities and alliances can also generate new forms of division and differentiation. All racialized groups face problems because of environmental racism, but Native Americans suffer particularly from cancer, Latinos from polluted air and pesticide exposure, African Americans from lead poisoning, Asian American and Pacific Islanders from underweight births and childhood malnutrition. Unemployment has hit African Americans harder than Asian Americans or Latinos, but women immigrants from Asia, Mexico, and Central America are over-represented in hazardous low-wage jobs.

Under these conditions, inter-ethnic anti-racism is emerging as a tactical necessity. This strategy does not erase purely national or racial identities, nor does it permanently transcend them. There is always room for more than one tactical stance in struggles for social justice, and ethnic nationalism and autonomous single-group struggles will always be legitimate and meaningful under some circumstances. But the current historical moment is generating new forms of struggle, forms eloquently described by scholar-activist Lisa Lowe as "alternative forms of practice that integrate yet move beyond those of cultural nationalism."

Eleanor Mill. Reprinted by permission of Mill NewsArt Syndicate.

Alliances across racial lines offer some obvious advantages. They produce strength in numbers; we are more powerful with allies than we would be alone. If we are there for other people's struggles, there is a greater likelihood that they will be there for us in the future if we need them. By standing up for someone else, we establish ourselves as people with empathy for the suffering of others; it shows that we will not turn our backs on people simply because they seem powerless.

Angela Davis points to the work of workers' centers like Asian Immigrant Women Advocates that address the whole lives of workers—not just their class, racial, or gender identities. These centers combine literacy classes with legal advice about domestic violence and divorce while they address issues about wages, hours, and working conditions.

Because there is no way to improve the lives of Asian American immigrant workers without attending to the concerns of Latinas who often work at their side, and because entrepreneurs from their own ethnic group are often part of the problem, these efforts inevitably lead to inter-ethnic alliances. They lead to cross-class alliances because there is no way to deal with domestic violence as a class-specific or race-specific problem. They also lead to the formation of temporary affinities and alliances across gender, class, and racial lines through tactics like consumer boycotts of goods created under unsafe or unfair working conditions.

Consider also some of the less obvious advantages of inter-ethnic anti-racism. Coordinated actions against racism enable aggrieved groups to focus on the fact of oppression itself rather than merely on the identities of the oppressed. Inter-ethnic anti-racism can shift the focus away from defensive concerns about "minority" disadvantages and toward an analysis of white "majority" advantages, thus helping to define the target.

This might show that racialized groups are not merely disadvantaged, but also taken advantage of. It might make visible the new forms of racialization created day after day in the present, not just those attributable to histories of slavery, conquest, genocide, immigrant exploitation, and class oppression.

Who's Got the Power?

In the final analysis, the most important reason for inter-ethnic anti-racism is that it provides the most effective way for us to see exactly how power works in the world. We will always misread and misunderstand our circumstances if we see things from only one perspective.

Solidarities based on identity are limited; solidarities based on identities are unlimited. All social movements need some form of organic solidarity. But people who must see themselves as exactly the same in order to wage a common struggle will be poorly prepared for struggles for social justice against a power structure that constantly creates new forms of differentiation among the oppressed.

Yet precisely because no unified identity encompasses anyone's social world, inter-ethnic anti-racist activism offers the opportunity to make struggles for social justice as mobile, fluid, and flexible as the new forms of oppression. They enable us to create places like the ones envisioned by Patrick Chamoiseau's narrator in *Texaco*, an epic novel about anti-racist struggle in Martinique: "those places in which no one could foresee our ability to unravel their History into our thousand stories."

| "Native-born U.S. citizens are being 'ethnically cleansed,' not by violence but by their own immigration policy."

Immigration Should Be Restricted

Paul Craig Roberts

In the following viewpoint, nationally syndicated columnist Paul Craig Roberts contends that mass immigration is endangering American society. More than one million immigrants move to the United States each year, he points out, and many of these immigrants are retaining their own cultures rather than adapting to American culture. Unless immigration is restricted, Roberts maintains, America's distinctive national culture will be threatened by dangerous racial and ethnic enclaves.

As you read, consider the following questions:

1. In Roberts's opinion, why did Democrats change U.S. immigration laws in 1965?
2. What privileges are granted to non-European immigrants but not to white Americans, according to the author?
3. According to Roberts, why did the city of Richmond, Virginia, have to remove a mural of Robert E. Lee?

Reprinted from "The Mass Displacement of European Americans: Extraordinary Change Produced by Immigration Policy," Paul Craig Roberts's syndicated column of June 21, 1999, by permission of Paul Craig Roberts and Creators Syndicate, Inc.

R ecently a federal judge wrote to me. The judge enclosed a list of new citizens for whom he had conducted a naturalization ceremony. He was astounded that among almost 100 new citizens there were only four or five Europeans.

Immigration policy has produced an extraordinary change in the ethnic composition of the U.S. population. Experts tell me it has been three decades since Europeans comprised a significant percentage of new citizens. In 1965 the Democrats, who lost the South, changed the immigration rules in order to build African, Asian and Hispanic constituencies that would vote Democratic.

In effect, native-born U.S. citizens are being "ethnically cleansed," not by violence but by their own immigration policy.

With the United States taking in 1.2 million immigrants annually, and with that number again entering illegally, cultural homogeneity has been the casualty.

Ethnic Divides

When I first came to Washington, D.C. 25 years ago, the only international-looking people one saw were in the diplomatic community. Now it is every third person. A person can now duplicate the experiences of world travel by just touring the neighborhoods inside the D.C. Beltway. It is much the same in most cities.

Recent immigrants who favor the melting pot are themselves alarmed. Yeh Ling-Ling, executive director of Diversity Alliance for a Sustainable America, believes we need a time-out from mass immigration in order to permit assimilation; otherwise, the United States will face ethnic divides that exceed those in Kosovo and the Balkans.

Yeh Ling-Ling reports that recently the Jewish principal of a predominately Latino school in San Fernando Valley was beaten unconscious by assailants who told him: "We don't want you here anymore, white principal."

Native-born white liberals use "diversity" to justify mass immigration beyond the ability of the melting pot to assimilate. But the unassimilated immigrants are not as tolerant of diversity as their white liberal spokespersons. Mario Obledo, co-founder of the Mexican American Legal Defense Fund, said on a radio program that Hispanics are going to take over all the political institutions of California and anyone who does not like it should leave.

In Dearborn, Mich., school fights have erupted between Arabs and non-Arabs, in New Jersey between Koreans and non-Koreans, in Maryland communities between Russian immigrants and native-born U.S. citizens, in Lexington, Ky., between blacks and Hispanics.

The Potential for Cultural Conflicts

If America loses the ability to assimilate the many (*plures*) into one united nation, it will become like Canada and other divided countries. When that happens, America will have lost its soul. It will then be a tribalistic country in which each group will selfishly seek its own ethnocentric norms, mores, and other foreign interests, eventually producing serious social and cultural conflicts, and probably even physical violence.

Alvin J. Schmidt, *The Menace of Multiculturalism*, 1997.

The formerly all-white community of Cupertino, Calif., has been so overrun by Chinese immigrants that the school board debated a Mandarin-immersion kindergarten class. Thai A. Nguyen-Khoa, a U.S. history teacher in San Francisco, has written about the conflict resulting from consigning Vietnamese immigrants to black housing projects.

There is a lot to be said in behalf of individual immigrants. I recently wrote about one, Juana Vasquez, a brave woman who stood up to the native-born white liberals who were acting out their fantasies by conducting a child sex abuse witch hunt in Wenatchee, Wash., and sending innocent parents to prison.

A sterling aspect of Third World immigrants is their lack of illusions about government. Unlike native-born liberals, non-European immigrants have been taught by experience to see government as the obstacle, not the path, to happiness.

When one encounters Third World immigrants as employees in government bureaucracies, they are often noticeably less officious than their white counterparts. In the end, the live-and-let-live Third World culture of bribery might be what saves us from increasingly intrusive government.

Immigrants Are "Preferred Minorities"

One downside to the massive non-European immigration is that, thanks to the liberals' civil rights policies, every one of these immigrants enters the United States as a "preferred minority" with legal privileges that native-born citizens of European origin do not have. For racial reasons unrelated to merit or competitive performance, every non-European immigrant is entitled to privileged consideration in university admissions, employment, promotions and government contracts.

It is impossible for the melting pot to work when new immigrants have a "preferred" status that the majority of native-born citizens do not have. People on whom legal privileges are conferred eventually feel like a privileged class and begin acting like one.

Mario Obledo is not the only one who believes native-born citizens are losing their country. Others see the demise of the native-born in a recent occurrence in Richmond, Va. There a city councilman, Sa'ad El-Amin, has forced the removal of a mural of Robert E. Lee, the most beloved of all Virginians.

When I was a kid even Northerners respected Robert E. Lee. Not a word was heard against him. But Sa'ad El-Amin compares Gen. Lee to Adolf Hitler.

Does this lack of good will toward "white culture" mean the portraits of George Washington and Thomas Jefferson will be removed from our currency and their historic homes, Mount Vernon and Monticello, closed? If mass immigration means the extinction of American culture, we had best rethink it.

Periodical Bibliography

The following articles have been selected to supplement the diverse views presented in this chapter. Addresses are provided for periodicals not indexed in the *Readers' Guide to Periodical Literature*, the *Alternative Press Index*, the *Social Sciences Index*, or the *Index to Legal Periodicals and Books*.

J. Jorge Klor de Alva and Cornel West	"Black-Brown Relations: Are Alliances Possible?" *Social Justice*, Summer 1997.
American Enterprise	"A Symposium: What Clinton's Year-Long Rap on Race Left Out," November/December 1998.
Edgar F. Beckham	"Diversity Opens Doors to All," *New York Times*, January 5, 1997.
Christopher Caldwell	"Fast Times at Annandale High," *Weekly Standard*, December 29, 1997. Available from 1211 Avenue of the Americas, New York, NY 10036.
Linda Chavez	"Multiculturalism Is Driving Us Apart," *USA Today Magazine*, May 1996.
Gary Delgado	"The Real Test Is Race," *Colorlines*, Fall 1999.
Christopher Edley Jr.	"Clinton's Initiative Is More than a Gabfest," *Washington Post National Weekly Edition*, December 15, 1997. Available from 1150 15th St. NW, Washington, DC 20071.
Glenn C. Loury	"To Get Beyond Therapy, an Agenda Is Needed," *Washington Post National Weekly Edition*, December 15, 1997.
Elizabeth Martinez	"Reinventing 'America,'" *Z Magazine*, December 1996.
Betsy Peoples	"A Simple Gesture," *Emerge*, September 1997. Available from One BET Plaza, 1900 W Pl. NE, Washington, DC 20018.
David Shipler	"Reflections on Race," *Tikkun*, January/February 1998.
Bill Wylie-Kellerman	"Exorcising an American Demon," *Sojourners*, March/April 1998.

For Further Discussion

Chapter 1

1. Deroy Murdock maintains that everyday American life is characterized by racial harmony rather than racial tension. Leonard Steinhorn and Barbara Diggs-Brown, on the other hand, contend that Americans are less racially tolerant than they pretend to be. What evidence do these authors present to support their conclusions? Whose argument is more convincing? Why?

2. Henry Louis Gates Jr. cites anti-Jewish passages in the Nation of Islam's *Secret Relationship Between Blacks and Jews* to help back his argument that anti-Semitism is increasing among African Americans. Clarence Page quotes the findings of a 1997 Kieran Mahoney poll to buttress his contention that black-Jewish relations are improving. In your opinion, which citation provides the strongest support for the author's conclusion? Explain.

3. Joseph Daleiden claims that one way to increase job opportunities for black citizens is to place more stringent restrictions on legal and illegal immigration. Elizabeth Martinez argues that African Americans and immigrant minorities should join forces to fight racist attitudes and secure more jobs for all. In your opinion, which author offers the most feasible solution to the controversy over job competition between blacks and immigrants?

Chapter 2

1. David K. Shipler incorporates testimony from interviews and discussions with blacks as well as survey statistics to support his conclusion that subtle forms of racism are a pervasive problem. Robert Weissberg contends that claims such as Shipler's are akin to a scientific theory, then analyzes and discredits the theory as part of his argument disproving the present-day harms of white racism. Which of these authors' approaches do you find more impressive? Explain.

2. Keeanga-Yamahtta Taylor argues that racial bias is a major factor in police officers' decisions to detain and search suspects. Walter Williams contends that race is simply a dependable indicator for police as they target criminal suspects. In your opinion, are there situations in which racial profiling is justified? Why or why not?

3. Edward Rush contends that polluters are more likely to locate in minority neighborhoods and expose disproportionate numbers

of blacks, Latinos, and Native Americans to toxins. Christopher H. Foreman Jr. maintains that such allegations of "environmental racism" are generally unwarranted. In each viewpoint, try to find two supporting arguments that you personally agree with. Why do you agree with them?

Chapter 3

1. Paul Butler argues that affirmative action and other race-based public policies help to compensate for past and ongoing discrimination against people of color. Charles Canady maintains that these race-based policies are actually a form of government-imposed discrimination. Which author do you agree with, and why?

2. William G. Bowen and Derek Bok discuss the findings from their survey of over 35,000 college students to support their contention that race-sensitive admissions policies are beneficial. Roger Clegg analyzes and debunks the claims of affirmative action supporters as part of his argument against race-sensitive policies. Which of these authors' techniques do you find more compelling? Why?

3. Jeff MacSwan contends that schools should employ bilingual education programs to ensure that immigrant students become proficient in English. Does Georgie Anne Geyer's viewpoint effectively refute MacSwan's argument? Why or why not?

Chapter 4

1. Michael S. Berliner and Gary Hull disagree with the Advisory Board to the President's Initiative on Race about the need to celebrate racial diversity. How do the arguments of these authors reflect differing views on the definition and nature of diversity? Explain your answer, using evidence from the viewpoints.

2. The viewpoints in this chapter include several recommendations for improving race relations. Consider each recommendation and then list arguments for and against each one. Note whether the arguments are based on facts, values, emotions, or other considerations. If you believe a recommendation should not be considered at all, explain why.

Organizations to Contact

The editors have compiled the following list of organizations concerned with the issues debated in this book. The descriptions are derived from materials provided by the organizations. All have publications or information available for interested readers. The list was compiled on the date of publication of the present volume; the information provided here may change. Be aware that many organizations take several weeks or longer to respond to inquiries, so allow as much time as possible.

American Civil Liberties Union (ACLU)
125 Broad St., 18th Floor, New York, NY 10004
(212) 549-2500 • fax: (212) 549-2646
website: www.aclu.org

The ACLU is a national organization that works to defend Americans' civil rights as guaranteed by the U.S. Constitution. The ACLU publishes and distributes policy statements, pamphlets, and the semiannual newsletter *Civil Liberties Alert*.

American Immigration Control Foundation (AICF)
PO Box 525, Monterey, VA 24465
(703) 468-2022 • fax: (703) 468-2024

The AICF is a research and educational organization whose primary goal is to promote a reasonable immigration policy based on national interests and needs. The foundation educates the public on what its members believe are the disastrous effects of uncontrolled immigration. It publishes the monthly newsletter *Border Watch* as well as several monographs and books on the historical, legal, and demographic aspects of immigration.

Amnesty International (AI)
322 Eighth Ave., New York, NY 10004-2400
(212) 807-8400 • (800) AMNESTY (266-3789)
fax: (212) 627-1451
website: www.amnesty-usa.org

Founded in 1961, AI is a grassroots activist organization that aims to free all nonviolent people who have been imprisoned because of their beliefs, ethnic origin, sex, color, or language. The *Amnesty International Report* is published annually, and other reports are available on-line and by mail.

Cato Institute
1000 Massachusetts Ave. NW, Washington, DC 20001-5403
(202) 842-0200 • fax: (202) 842-3490
e-mail: cato@cato.org • website: www.cato.org
The Cato Institute is a libertarian public policy research foundation dedicated to limiting the role of government and protecting individual liberties. It researches claims of discrimination and opposes affirmative action. The institute offers numerous publications, including the *Cato Journal*, the bimonthly newsletter *Cato Policy Report*, and the quarterly magazine *Regulation*.

Center for the Study of Popular Culture (CSPC)
9911 W. Pico Blvd., Suite 1290, Los Angeles, CA 90035
(310) 843-3699 • fax: (310) 843-3692
website: www.cspc.org
CSPC is a conservative educational organization that addresses topics such as political correctness, cultural diversity, and discrimination. Its civil rights project promotes equal opportunity for all individuals and provides legal assistance to citizens challenging affirmative action. The center publishes four magazines: *Heterodoxy*, *Defender, Report Card*, and *COMINT.*

Citizens' Commission on Civil Rights (CCCR)
2000 M St. NW, Suite 400, Washington, DC 20036
(202) 659-5565 • fax: (202) 223-5302
e-mail: citizens@cccr.org • website: www.cccr.org
CCCR monitors the federal government's enforcement of antidiscrimination laws and promotes equal opportunity for all. It publishes reports on affirmative action and desegregation as well as the book *One Nation Indivisible: The Civil Rights Challenge for the 1990s.*

Commission for Racial Justice (CRJ)
700 Prospect Ave., Cleveland, OH 44115-1110
(216) 736-2100 • fax: (216) 736-2171
CRJ was formed in 1963 by the United Church of Christ in response to racial tensions gripping the nation at that time. Its goal is a peaceful, dignified society where all men and women are equal. CRJ publishes various documents and books, such as *Racism and the Pursuit of Racial Justice* and *A National Symposium on Race and Housing in the United States: Challenges for the 21st Century.*

Heritage Foundation
214 Massachusetts Ave. NE, Washington, DC 20002-4999
(202) 546-4400 • fax: (202) 546-8328
e-mail: info@heritage.org • website: www.heritage.org

The foundation is a conservative public policy research institute that advocates free-market principles, individual liberty, and limited government. It believes the private sector, not government, should be relied upon to ease social problems and to improve the status of minorities. The Heritage Foundation publishes the quarterly *Policy Review* and the bimonthly newsletter *Heritage Today* as well as numerous monographs, books, and papers.

Hispanic Policy Development Project (HPDP)
1001 Connecticut Ave. NW, Suite 901, Washington, DC 20036
(202) 822-8414 • fax: (202) 822-9120

HPDP encourages the analysis of public policies affecting Hispanics in the United States, particularly the education, training, and employment of Hispanic youth. It publishes a number of books and pamphlets, including *Together Is Better: Building Strong Partnerships Between Schools and Hispanic Parents*.

National Association for the Advancement of Colored People (NAACP)
4805 Mt. Hope Dr., Baltimore, MD 21215-3297
(410) 358-8900 • fax: (410) 486-9257

The NAACP is the oldest and largest civil rights organization in the United States. Its principal objective is to ensure the political, educational, social, and economic equality of minorities. It publishes the magazine *Crisis* ten times a year as well as a variety of newsletters, books, and pamphlets.

National Network for Immigrant and Refugee Rights (NNIRR)
310 Eighth St., Suite 307, Oakland, CA 94607
(510) 465-1984 • fax: (510) 465-1885
e-mail: nnirr@igc.apc.org • website: www.nnirr.org

The network includes community, church, labor, and legal groups committed to the cause of equal rights for all immigrants. These groups work to end discrimination and unfair treatment of illegal immigrants and refugees. The network publishes a monthly newsletter, *Network News*.

National Urban League
120 Wall St., 8th Floor, New York, NY 10005
(212) 558-5300 • fax: (212) 344-5332
website: www.nul.org
A community service agency, the National Urban League aims to
eliminate institutional racism in the United States. It also provides services for minorities who experience discrimination in employment, housing, welfare, and other areas. It publishes the report *The Price: A Study of the Costs of Racism in America* and the
annual *State of Black America*.

Poverty and Race Research Action Council (PRRAC)
3000 Connecticut Ave. NW, Suite 200, Washington, DC 20008
(202) 387-9887 • fax: (202) 387-0764
e-mail: info@prrac.org
The Poverty and Race Research Action Council is a nonpartisan,
national, not-for-profit organization convened by major civil
rights, civil liberties, and antipoverty groups. PRRAC's purpose is
to link social science research to advocacy work in order to suc-
cessfully address problems at the intersection of race and poverty.
Its bimonthly publication, *Poverty and Race*, often includes articles
on race- and income-based inequities in the United States.

The Prejudice Institute
Stephens Hall Annex, TSU, Towson, MD 21204-7097
(410) 830-2435 • fax: (410) 830-2455
The Prejudice Institute is a national research center concerned
with violence and intimidation motivated by prejudice. It conducts research, supplies information on model programs and legislation, and provides education and training to combat prejudicial violence. The Prejudice Institute publishes research reports,
bibliographies, and the quarterly newsletter *Forum*.

United States Commission on Civil Rights
624 Ninth St. NW, Suite 500, Washington, DC 20425
(202) 376-7533 • publications: (202) 376-8128
A fact-finding body, the commission reports directly to Congress
and the president on the effectiveness of equal opportunity laws
and programs. A catalog of its numerous publications can be obtained from its Publication Management Division.

Bibliography of Books

Teja Arboldea — *In the Shadow of Race: Growing Up as a Multiethnic, Multicultural, and "Multiracial" American.* Mahwah, NJ: Lawrence Erlbaum, 1998.

James A. Banks — *An Introduction to Multicultural Education.* Boston: Allyn and Bacon, 1999.

William G. Bowen and Derek Curtis Bok — *The Shape of the River: Long-Term Consequences of Considering Race in College and University Admissions.* Princeton, NJ: Princeton University Press, 1998.

Maria Estela Brisk — *Bilingual Education: From Compensatory to Quality Education.* Mahwah, NJ: Lawrence Erlbaum, 1997.

Karen Brodkin — *How Jews Became White Folks and What That Says About Race in America.* New Brunswick, NJ: Rutgers University Press, 1998.

Jim Carnes — *Us and Them: A History of Intolerance in America.* New York: Oxford University Press, 1999.

Farai Chideya — *The Color of Our Future.* New York: William Morrow, 1999.

Jonathan Coleman — *Long Way to Go: Black and White in America.* New York: Atlantic Monthly Press, 1997.

Ellis Cose — *Color-Blind: Seeing Beyond Race in a Race-Obsessed World.* New York: HarperCollins, 1997.

George E. Curry, ed. — *The Affirmative Action Debate.* Reading, MA: Addison-Wesley, 1996.

Harlon L. Dalton — *Racial Healing: Confronting the Fear Between Blacks and Whites.* New York: Doubleday, 1995.

Richard Delgado — *When Equality Ends: Stories About Race and Resistance.* Boulder, CO: Westview Press, 1999.

Dinesh D'Souza — *The End of Racism: Principles for a Multiracial Society.* New York: Free Press, 1995.

Jennifer L. Eberhardt and Susan T. Fiske, eds. — *Confronting Racism: The Problem and the Response.* Thousand Oaks, CA: Sage, 1998.

Joe R. Feagin and Hernan Vera — *White Racism: The Basics.* New York: Routledge, 1995.

Paul Harris — *Black Rage Confronts the Law.* New York: New York University Press, 1997.

Jon Hurwitz and Mark Peffley, eds. — *Perception and Prejudice: Race and Politics in the United States.* New Haven, CT: Yale University Press, 1998.

Kevin R. Johnson	*How Did You Get to Be Mexican? A White/Brown Man's Search for Identity.* Philadelphia: Temple University Press, 1999.
Paul Kivel	*Uprooting Racism: How White People Can Work for Racial Justice.* Philadelphia: New Society Publishers, 1996.
Robert G. Lee	*Orientals: Asian Americans in Popular Culture.* Philadelphia: Temple University Press, 1999.
Eric Liu	*The Accidental Asian: Notes of a Native Speaker.* New York: Random House, 1998.
Don C. Locke	*Increasing Multicultural Understanding: A Comprehensive Model.* Thousand Oaks, CA: Sage, 1998.
Paula Mitchell Marks	*In a Barren Land: American Indian Dispossession and Survival.* New York: William Morrow, 1998.
Elizabeth Martinez	*De Colores Means All of Us: Latina Views for a Multi-Colored Century.* Cambridge, MA: South End Press, 1998.
Laughlin McDonald	*The Rights of Racial Minorities.* New York: Puffin, 1998.
Larry L. Naylor	*American Culture: Myth and Reality of a Culture of Diversity.* Westport, CT: Bergin & Garvey, 1998.
David Palumbo-Liu	*Asian/American: Historical Crossings of a Racial Frontier.* Stanford, CA: Stanford University Press, 1999.
Elaine Pascoe	*Racial Prejudice: Why Can't We Overcome.* Danbury, CT: Franklin Watts, 1997.
Richard J. Payne	*Getting Beyond Race: The Changing American Culture.* Boulder, CO: Westview Press, 1998.
Patricia Raybon	*My First White Friend: Confessions on Race, Love, and Forgiveness.* New York: Penguin, 1997.
Jack Salzman and Cornel West, eds.	*Struggles in the Promised Land: Toward a History of Black-Jewish Relations in the United States.* New York: Oxford University Press, 1997.
Alvin J. Schmidt	*The Menace of Multiculturalism: Trojan Horse in America.* Westport, CT: Praeger, 1997.
David K. Shipler	*A Country of Strangers: Blacks and Whites in America.* New York: Knopf, 1997.
Shelby Steele	*A Dream Deferred: The Second Betrayal of Black Freedom in America.* New York: HarperCollins, 1998.

Leonard Steinhorn and
Barbara Diggs-Brown

By the Color of Our Skin: The Illusion of Integration and the Reality of Race. New York: Penguin, 1999.

Beverly Daniel Tatum

"Why Are All the Black Kids Sitting Together in the Cafeteria?" and Other Conversations About Race. New York: BasicBooks, 1997.

Thandeka

Learning to Be White: Money, Race, and God in America. New York: Continuum, 1999.

Paul L. Wachtel

Race in the Mind of America: Breaking the Vicious Circle Between Blacks and Whites. New York: Routledge, 1999.

James Waller

Face to Face: The Changing State of Racism Across America. New York: Insight Books, 1998.

Tom Wicker

Tragic Failure: Racial Integration in America. New York: William Morrow, 1996.

Patricia J. Williams

Seeing a Color-Blind Future: The Paradox of Race. New York: Noonday Press, 1998.

W.D. Wright

Racism Matters. Westport, CT: Praeger, 1998.

Index